MW01074874

THE ORVIS POCKET GUIDE TO
FLY FISHING FOR BASS

Books by William G. Tapply

FICTION:
The Brady Coyne Novels
First Light: The First Ever Brady Coyne/J.W. Jackson Mystery
(by Philip R. Craig and William G. Tapply)

NONFICTION:
Those Hours Spent Outdoors: Reflections on Hunting and Fishing
Opening Day and Other Neuroses
Home Water Near and Far: A Fly Fisherman's Explorations
Sportsman's Legacy
A Fly-Fishing Life
Bass Bug Fishing
Upland Days: Fifty Years of Bird Hunting in New England
Pocket Water: Confessions of a Restless Angler
The Elements of Mystery Fiction: Writing a Modern Whodunit

THE ORVIS POCKET GUIDE TO
Fly Fishing for Bass

Where, When, and How to Catch Largemouths and Smallmouths

WILLIAM G. TAPPLY

The Lyons Press
Guilford, Connecticut
An Imprint of The Globe Pequot Press

Copyright ©2002 by William G. Tapply

All rights reserved. No part of this book may be reproduced or transmitted in any form by any means, electronic or mechanical, including photocopying and recording, or by any information storage and retrieval system, except as may be expressly permitted by the 1976 Copyright Act or in writing from the publisher. Requests for permission should be addressed to The Globe Pequot Press, P.O. Box 480, Guilford, CT 06437.

The Lyons Press is an imprint of The Globe Pequot Press.

Printed in Canada.

10 9 8 7 6 5 4 3 2 1

Library of Congress Cataloging-in-Publication Data is available on file.

ISBN 1-58574-795-5

CONTENTS

ACKNOWLEDGMENTS

The countless men and women who have shared their boats and their wisdom and their jokes and their sandwiches with me during fifty years of fly fishing for bass deserve all the credit for making this book possible. I couldn't begin to mention them all, but special thanks go to: Andy Gill, Will Ryan, Cliff Hauptman, Art Scheck, John Likakis, Vicki Stiefel, and Mike, Melissa, and Sarah Tapply.

Writers never work alone. I have been blessed with astute and understanding editors throughout my career. They have held me to high standards and made me a better writer. Special thanks to: Nick Lyons, Jay Cassell, Slaton White, Duncan Barnes, Phil Monahan, Art Scheck, John Likakis, Joe Healy, Tom Rosenbauer, and Jim Babb.

My father was my No. 1 fishing partner and my writing mentor and all-round best friend for sixty years. H. G. "Tap" Tapply died on January 24, 2002. I only hope that this book is up to his standards.

THE LURE OF FLY-ROD BASS FISHING

Black bass—largemouths and smallmouths—are native only to North America. Today, after decades of transplanting and centuries of natural migration, they thrive in all of the lower forty-eight states. Very few Americans need to drive more than an hour to find decent bass fishing. Virtually every weedy pond, rocky lake, man-made impoundment, lazy creek, and big river in America harbors a healthy population of naturally reproducing largemouths or smallmouths. Many waters hold both.

Bass have become America's most popular game-fish, and with good reason. They strike aggressively, fight hard, jump eagerly, reproduce wantonly, and grow large.

Bass eat any living thing they can catch—insects, worms, lizards, crustaceans, other fish, and even an occasional small animal or bird. When he's in an eating mood—as he generally is—a hungry bass rarely snubs his nose at anything that's digestible—or that even looks digestible. You can catch bass on just about any fly you tie to the end of your line.

High-tech bass fishing has become a big business in America. If you've ever tuned in a Saturday-morning cable channel, you know what I mean. The professional bassers would lead you to believe that if you want to catch bass, you need a fistful of rods, a

Author with a largemouth that took a bug chugged through a patch of lily pads.

steamer trunk full of lures, and a streamlined bass boat built for speed, with a big motor on the transom, a foot-operated electric motor up front, a live well, and an electronic fishfinder.

Everybody's entitled to his own version of fun, but when I go bass fishing, I just rig up my fly rod, tie on a generic streamer or floating bug, climb into my canoe or float tube, and cast into the shallow water where bass like to go hunting. I suppose there are times when I might catch more or bigger bass with crankbaits or buzzbaits or spinnerbaits or stickbaits, but I usually catch enough bass on flies to satisfy myself. This book isn't about catching the most or the biggest bass.

This book is about the fun of using a fly rod to cast lightweight lures made from feathers and fur for bass, which is probably the oldest form of hook-and-line fishing in North America. It's a quiet, low-tech, unhurried, non-competitive, uncomplicated method of fishing, and it always surprises me to meet devout fly-rod anglers who've never tried it.

Lobbing out something big and buggy with a long pole and dragging it across the surface of a pond, lake, or creek is an American invention. In 1741 William Bartram observed the Seminole Indians in Florida catch largemouth bass (which Bartram called "trout") on a "bob." Undoubtedly the Seminoles had been doing it that way for many generations before Europeans set foot in North America.

This big mid-summer largemouth inhaled a streamer fished around a jumble of rocks. Credit: Will Ryan

"Two people are in a little canoe," Bartram reported, "one sitting in the stern to steer, and the other near the bow, having a rod ten or twelve feet in length, to one end of which is tied a strong line, about twenty inches in length, to which is fastened three large hooks, back to back. These are fixed very securely, and tied with the white hair of a deer's tail, shreds of a red garter, and some particoloured feathers, all which form a tuft or tassel nearly as large as one's fist, and entirely cover and conceal the hooks; that is called a 'bob.' The steersman paddles softly, and proceeds slowly along shore, keeping parallel to it, at a distance just sufficient to admit the fisherman to reach the edge of the floating weeds along shore; he now ingeniously swings the bob backwards and forwards, just above the surface and sometimes tips the water with it; when the unfortunate cheated trout [sic] instantly springs from under the weeds and seizes the prey."

Substitute an 8-weight graphite fly rod with a line to match, a 9-foot tapered leader, and a deer-hair or feathered fly that is twitched and burbled across or just under the surface of the water, and Bartram is describing modern-day fly-rod fishing for bass.

The Seminole Indians fished for food, not sport. Everglades largemouths were available and abundant. If bob fishing hadn't been an effective technique for catching them, those Native Americans would have found a better way.

Still, one can't help but think that they had fun doing it.

Bass-bugging before sunup brings largemouths to the surface.

Early American anglers brought their European traditions to the New World. They fished for sport, and sport meant trout and salmon. They were slow to discover the gamy qualities of smallmouth and largemouth bass, and when they did, they employed trout flies and trout methods to catch them. Dr. James Henshall's *Book of the Black Bass* (1881) was the first to focus exclusively on bass fishing. His brief chapter on flies describes only insect imitations. His list of "bass" flies is limited to wet and dry patterns developed for trout fishing. Still, Henshall hit the bull's-eye on the subject of fly selection: "Where fish are plentiful and in a 'biting mood,'" he wrote, "almost any fly, be it never so rudely tied, and of the least possible resemblance to any thing in the insect creation, will be successful."

After the turn of the century, fly rodding for bass became wildly popular, thanks to the discovery that bass loved to hit surface lures concocted from feathers, fur, and cork that could be cast with a fly rod. Fly-rod bass pioneers such as Ernest Peckinpaugh, Orley Tuttle, and Joe Messinger designed and marketed floaters that, not surprisingly, caught lots of fish.

In the latter half of the twentieth century and into the present time, fly fishermen such as Ray Bergman, Joe Brooks, Tom Nixon, John Alden Knight, Charley Waterman, Dave Whitlock, Jack Ellis, Will Ryan, Harry Murray, and many others have invented fly-rod lures, studied bass behavior, developed specialized techniques, and written extensively on the subject. Today's manufacturers offer wide ranges of rods, lines,

The warming waters of springtime get smallmouths particularly hungry.
Credit: Will Ryan

flies, and other fly-fishing equipment specifically designed for bass.

There are three ways to catch bass on flies: on the surface, just under the surface, and near the bottom. Bass flies that are designed to float are called bugs, even though they don't necessarily resemble insects. Subsurface bass flies are called streamers, although many of them bear little resemblance to the classic streamer flies anglers use for trout and salmon. Bottom-bumping flies are tied with lead eyes or other weight. In rivers, and sometimes on lakes and ponds, nymphs and dry flies meant for trout work for bass.

The fly rod may not be the most efficient weapon for catching the most bass or the biggest bass, although I'm convinced that sometimes it is. Nevertheless, anyone who's tried it will tell you that casting flies for bass in shallow water is loads of fun—and that fishing with floating bugs is the most fun of all. As A. J. McClane wrote, "I suppose the peculiar fascination bass bugging has is in the strike. To see a heavy fish rise from under the lily pads or slip out from under a dense growth of weeds to smash at a floating bug is the most tense moment an angler can experience at the end of any search."

Catching bass on the fly rod is relatively straightforward, low-tech, and simple—but it's not simplistic. Doing it effectively and consistently may be less than science, but it's more than luck.

Luck, of course, always helps.

It also helps to have an assortment of good flies, along with the right equipment and enough skill to use

Smallmouth bass are sometimes called "bronzebacks." Credit: Fred Bobson

it properly. It helps a lot to know where bass hang out and when you're likely to find them in the mood to slurp in a fly. These are among the matters we'll explore in this book.

CHAPTER ONE

BASS IN SHALLOW WATER

One of the reasons bass fishing has become so popular is that they live in virtually every body of fresh water in the lower forty-eight states, and they usually lurk in shallow water where the angler can fish for them effectively. Smallmouths coexist with lake trout and landlocked salmon in cold, deep Northern lakes and with rainbow, brown, and brook trout in quick-moving rivers and streams. Largemouths find virtually all warmwater lakes, ponds, reservoirs, rivers, creeks, and sloughs hospitable. About the only

In weedy coves fallen timber holds both largemouths and smallmouths.
Credit: Will Ryan

reason why a body of fresh water might not hold bass is because the fish have not found a way to migrate into it, and nobody has yet dumped in a bucketful.

Bass live just about everywhere for two reasons: They can tolerate a wide range of water conditions and temperatures, and they eat anything that moves.

The challenge for the bass fisherman is just this simple: Locate some water where bass live (almost everywhere), tie something to the end of your line (almost anything), cast it out there (however awkwardly), and make it move. Everything beyond that is refinement.

The more refined you become, of course, the more bass you'll catch.

Fishermen have been studying bass behavior, trying to understand what makes them tick, since Dr. Henshall wrote *Book of the Black Bass* in 1881. Now, more than a century later, no one has yet been able to prove that he knows how bass think. We use words like "hungry" and "angry" and "shy" and "opportunistic"—words that we humans use to describe how our own minds work—because they seem to account for the bass behavior we can observe.

What we actually know about bass corresponds to what we know about the behavior of all wild creatures: Everything they do is intended to promote their survival both as individuals and as a species. In other words, they eat, they try to avoid getting eaten, and they spawn.

Bass have evolved into finely tuned predators. They devote most of their lives to locating, stalking, catching, and devouring food. Efficient predators like bass hunt in places where their prey is most abundant and easiest to capture, and they eat whatever they happen to find there. A list of bass foods would really be an unabridged compendium of all creatures that live in and near water, but close to the top of any list would be shallow-water creatures—small fish of all species (including baby bass), frogs and other amphibians, aquatic insects, leeches, worms, and various land-lubbing critters that fall or are blown onto the water.

The more vulnerable the prey, the better bass like it. Like all creatures, bass live by nature's equation: They survive and prosper when they can ingest the maximum nourishment with the minimum expenditure of energy. Bass are consistently found in shallow water (where it's the most fun to fish for them) because they find a lot of food there. Baitfish, leeches, and tadpoles tend to congregate around shallow-water weedbeds. Frogs, salamanders, and other amphibians spend most of their time in the water, and they never stray far from shore. Damselflies, dragonflies, mayflies, and other aquatic insects hatch in or near shallow water. Crayfish hide among shallow-water rocks. Worms live in the mud. Terrestrial insects such as grasshoppers, beetles, crickets, caterpillars, and moths, as well as creatures like mice, moles, and baby birds, plop onto the water from the trees and grass that overhang the shoreline.

Bass seek cover so they can hide from their own predators while they lie in ambush for prey, and they want comfortable water temperatures and shelter from sources of discomfort such as bright sun. Most of the time they find everything they want in or near shallow water. Because so much of their prey appears on or near the water's surface, bass are always looking up. In fact, they are designed to feed on or near the top; bass's eyes are located toward the top of their heads. If the water is clear enough for them to see to the surface, they'll happily shoot up from 10 or 15 feet deep to hit something on or near the top.

It's undoubtedly true that bass do most of their feeding underwater, because that's where they find their staples—baitfish, leeches, crayfish, and nymphs. If they're in an eating frame of mind, bass eagerly suck in streamers fished a foot or so deep. When they're lurking in deeper water, you might have to go deeper with weighted flies on a sink-tip line, although for most fly-rod bass anglers, that is a last resort.

Luckily for fly fishermen, both largemouths and smallmouths are usually found in shallow water where they're happy to feed off the top. In fact, bass have learned that any prey appearing on or near the surface is probably out of its natural element and therefore more vulnerable and easier to catch than what lives deep in the water. A baitfish thrashing near the surface must be injured or disoriented. Any insect or terrestrial creature that falls onto the water is quite helpless. Amphibians such as frogs are relatively poor swimmers, a nourishing bellyful, and no match for hungry bass.

With bass, nothing is absolute. I've found river-dwelling smallmouths sucking in nymphs or gobbling mayflies or windblown terrestrials as selectively as brown trout. Sometimes bass refuse to eat

Smallmouths lurk in shallow water until the heat of summer warms it up.
Credit: Fred Bobson

anything except a particularly abundant prey species such as soft-shelled crayfish. Sometimes they just aren't hungry.

Typically, however, bass are on the prowl for any nourishing mouthful they can find. Unlike trout anglers, we bass fishermen don't need to wait for and match a hatch to entice a fish to strike, nor do we need to imitate whatever a fish might've eaten most recently or even what it's accustomed to finding in and on the water.

In fact, we don't need to imitate anything to catch bass consistently. Bass are confirmed opportunists. They go for anything that *suggests* food. As author and naturalist Paul Schullery has said, "Bass are such admirable omnivores that they will eat almost anything if they're hungry, or disturbed, enough."

A canoe is a good way to navigate shallow water for bass. Credit: Will Ryan

Bass hunt by both sight and sound. They have a highly developed lateral line—their "hearing" organ—and can detect vibration and motion from long distances. If a grasshopper, dragonfly, moth, mouse, or frog—or bass bug—falls onto calm water and sits there twitching and struggling, every bass within 20 feet or so will hear it. If a school of baitfish approaches, or if a crayfish scurries for cover, nearby bass sense it. If it sounds like it might be good to eat, one of them will usually swim over to investigate. Then, if it looks alive and nourishing, whether or not it resembles anything he's ever seen before, he'll engulf it without bothering to inquire about its ancestry.

There is no evidence that bass refuse to strike a lure because it's the "wrong" shape or color (although sometimes, for reasons we don't understand, they do seem to respond to some flies and ignore others). Bass are conditioned to assume that anything they find wiggling, darting, or twitching in or on the water is alive and therefore good to eat, even if they've never seen anything like it before.

This is not to say that bass are always mindlessly aggressive, although often they appear to be exactly that. They are always alert for predators and quick to flee, and there are times when they seem to have little interest in eating. At such times, however, they can often be teased, seduced, angered, or tormented into striking.

During their spawning season, bass shift their attention from eating to protecting their territory, and they become, if anything, even more aggressive. Any alien that invades their sacred space, including a big streamer or a noisy bass bug, is, by their definition, an enemy that must be attacked and chased away or destroyed.

Thumb through today's fly-fishing catalogs, and you'll discover that bass flies come in an overwhelming variety of sizes, shapes, colors, and designs. There are poppers, chuggers, sliders, and divers made from deer hair, cork, balsa, hard and soft foam, silicone, synthetic tubing, and plastic. There are crayfish and worm and leech imitations and all manner of streamer flies both weighted and unweighted. Many are clever and precise imitations of actual bass prey.

The unwary bass angler might feel compelled to buy several of everything in each size and color available, on the theory that you never know what the bass might want at any given time on any particular body of water.

This nice largemouth lived in a weedy cove.

This theory often proves useful for trout fishermen. Trout really can be agonizingly selective.

It's pretty much nonsense, however, for the bass fisherman. What bass usually "want" is something—anything—that's alive, easy to capture, and nourishing, and that's what—and *only* what—an effective bass fly needs to suggest to trigger the fish's predatory impulse. One of the most productive tournament bass lures ever invented, for example, is the plastic worm. It's typically purple and 8 or 10 inches long, and it resembles nothing in nature, but the professional bassers make a worm wiggle and slither in ways that bass find irresistible.

Fancy, highly imitative bass flies rarely catch more bass than generic, suggestive ones do, although they probably catch more fishermen. A lot of technique goes into to catching bass on the fly rod, and you can consider many criteria when selecting a fly, but imitating specific bass prey is at the bottom of the list.

CHAPTER TWO

BASS ON TOP

We'll look first at floating flies—bass bugs—because there's nothing in all of fly fishing that matches that heart-stopping implosion a big bass makes when he swirls at the surface to suck in bug. When conditions are at all favorable, I always fish with bugs.

Every bass-bug aficionado I know has his favorite bug. He ties it on because . . . well, because he's had good luck with it in the past, because he likes the way it acts on the water, because he enjoys casting it, and sometimes because he made it himself. None gives much thought to imitating anything particular, although they all believe that the way they manipulate their bug makes it more or less imitate bass prey in general.

I happen to do most of my bass bugging with the deer-hair popper my father invented about fifty years ago. Tap's Bug resembles no natural bass food. Dad designed his bug to meet the needs of the fisherman, not the imagined appetites of bass. It's easy to tie, floats well, casts easily on midweight fly rods, and can be made to burble, gurgle, plop, glug, and slither in ways that smallmouths and largemouths in all types of water consistently find irresistible.

Usually when I go bass fishing, I just tie on a Tap's Bug and fish with it all day, unless a pickerel or a pike

Tap's Bug—an old favorite.

tears it up or I break it off in the bushes or in the mouth of a big bass. When that happens, I tie on another one.

When the bass show little interest in a Tap's Bug, and I'm not yet ready to concede that a streamer or a jig is the answer, I experiment with different bug designs. This makes me feel as if I'm doing something constructive, and I usually do it with a purpose in mind. When I do try different bugs, I have logical reasons, although not much science, for doing so.

CONDITIONS TO CONSIDER

My choice of bugs depends on the conditions I encounter on the water, not on the particular food I imagine bass are looking for.

- In *shallow, flat-calm water*, I worry that my bug might spook fish when it hits the water. So I cast smallish, soft-bodied bugs that land with a natural-sounding, quiet *splat* rather than an attention-getting *splash,* and I prefer bugs with rounded faces that gurgle and burble seductively rather than those with flat faces that pop loudly.
- When I'm casting to *small pockets and tight holes* such as openings in a bed of lily pads or under overhanging bushes or among the limbs of water-logged trees, where the bug must do its work without being moved away from the hotspot, I like a design that vibrates and wiggles when I give it just the slightest twitch. Rubber arms and legs and hairy or splayed hackle-feather or marabou tails impart subtle, lifelike movements to a bug while it rests on the water.
- When *a breeze riffles the surface*, I tie on something big and loud to command a bass's attention, such as a flat-nosed deer-hair bug or a hard-bodied lure with a cupped face that will move water and send out strong vibrations.
- When I'm casting over *dropoffs, shoals, sunken weedbeds, and other cover in deeper water*, I like big, low-riding bugs with tails made from marabou or rabbit strips and Krystal Flash or Flashabou to flutter, pulsate, and glitter under the surface while the cork or deer-hair body chugs along on top.
- When I'm casting to *water that's blanketed with lily pads*, I tie on a large, lightweight foam bug with a weedguard. I want it to slither over the

weeds without getting fouled, but I want it to draw the attention of any bass lurking in the shadow of the pads.

- When all else is equal, I prefer smaller (Size 2) bugs in natural colors (gray, white, or tan) for smallmouths, and bigger (Size 2/0) in combinations of white, yellow, green, and red for largemouths. On dark days and at twilight I go with darker colors. For nighttime bugging, I like all-black, which presents a sharp silhouette to a bass looking up at it, with a white face for my own eyes. I doubt if *size and color* actually make much of a difference for either species, but when the fishing is slow, this is how I think.

River-dwelling smallmouths love large attractor dry flies such as these.

When we analyze the qualities of a good bass bug, we must look beyond the baseline question, "Will it catch bass?" We already know the answer to that one.

BASS BUG CHARACTERISTICS

Here, in their order of importance, are what most bass-bug fishermen consider to be the characteristics of an effective bug:

- *Aerodynamics.* A good bass bug is lightweight and streamlined. It offers little air resistance when you cast it. It does not twist the leader or plane or flutter off target. You should be able to cast it 50 feet with a tight loop, pinpoint accuracy, and minimal false casting on a medium-weight fly rod, and you should be able to do it all day without tearing your rotator cuff. Most commercial bugs come with more legs and arms and tails and other air-resistant materials than they need. Cut off some of that stuff, and you'll have a bug that bass like just as much but which casts far more easily.
- *Noise.* Burbles and gurgles are more lifelike and, under most conditions, attract bass better than either sharp pops or no noise at all. The angler should be able to impart a variety of noises, from soft and subtle to loud and attention grabbing, to a good bug.
- *Behavior.* The best bass bugs are never absolutely motionless. When they're twitched and retrieved, they vibrate with life. Between twitches, they quiver and shiver, shudder and flutter. A bug with

rubber legs, hackle, hair, or feathers—just enough to give the bug the illusion of life when it's sitting quietly on the water but not enough to make it hard to cast—will entice reluctant bass to gulp it in.

- *Touchdown.* The way a bug falls upon the water will either attract or frighten any bass in the area, particularly if you've read the water accurately, executed a pinpoint cast, and dropped your bug onto his nose. Most natural bass prey hit the water with a muffled *plop* or *splat,* not a startling *splash.* Bass bugs should, too.

- *Feel.* All fish feel with their mouths, but the bass's mouth is especially sensitive. If a bass takes something into his mouth that doesn't feel right, he'll eject it so fast that you'd swear he struck short and missed it completely. Bass hit anything that looks edible. Only if it *feels* edible, however, will they hold it in their mouth long enough for the fisherman to react and set the hook.

- *Buoyancy.* Bass bugs are supposed to float. If they absorb water and begin sinking after a few casts, they are inefficient regardless of their other qualities. A bug that rides low in the water with its belly submerged, however, offers the bass a more natural profile, emits more lifelike, fish-attracting noises, and creates more enticing wiggles and twitches than a high-rider that floats entirely atop the surface.

- *Hook.* The gape, or "bite," of the hook should be wide relative to the size of the bug for consisten hookups. The point should be sharp, and the barb should be mashed down. Barbless hooks not only penetrate better than those with barbs, but they also enable you to unhook and release your fish— not to mention yourself or your partner, should you have a casting accident—quickly and harmlessly.

- *Size.* In general, the ancient wisdom that large-mouths prefer bigger bugs than smallmouths seems to hold true. But when the fish are uncooperative and the water is flat calm, I have often found that small, even panfish-sized, bugs entice more strikes from both species. On riffled water and at night an outsized bug usually draws more attention.

- *Shape and color.* These are the features generally touted in catalogs, and in much bass-bugging literature, to distinguish one bug from another. Catalogs assume their readers have a trout-fishing, hatch-matching mentality, so they emphasize imitation, and they imply that you need the "right" bug, meaning the one that imitates the prey species the bass are supposed to be looking for at that moment, to catch them. That's why so many commercial bugs are shaped, colored, and named for the prey they theoretically represent—diving frog, wounded minnow, fluttering moth, etc. On the water where it counts, however, color or shape or even both of these factors taken together are less significant than any one of those other qualities. The shape of a bug needn't imitate anything.

Overall shape matters because it affects how well the bug casts and how it behaves on the water.

Some fishermen theorize that a long, thin bug resembles baitfish and should be fished around boulders, along the edges of weedbeds, and over points and dropoffs, and a short, fat bug resembles the various pudgy terrestrial species that fall onto the water near shore. Thinking this way gives these anglers confidence in their choice of bug, which encourages them to fish it thoroughly and carefully. This will produce the kind of results that reinforces their thinking.

My strategy on color is to use a bug I can see on the water, because I haven't noticed that the bass give a hoot. They see only the belly of a floating bug. Everything above the water's surface is a blurry silhouette from the bass's perspective.

- *Durability.* Bass are toothless creatures, so a good bug should survive dozens of chomps. If your bug frays, comes unraveled, or falls apart after a few fish have glommed onto it, it was poorly made. If you encounter toothy fish such as pike and pickerel (which smash bass bugs with heart-stopping enthusiasm), all bets are off.
- *Weedlessness.* A bug that slithers around, over, and through weeds and snags allows the fisherman to cast closer to the places where bass lurk. A properly constructed weedguard will not significantly reduce your chances of hooking any bass that takes your bug in his mouth. The most effective weedguard is made from one or two strands of monofi-

ament attached to the rear of the hook, looped around the bend, and fastened behind the eye.

- *Imitativeness.* Underwater flies and lures that resemble specific prey—common species of baitfish and crayfish in particular—arguably work better than generic, suggestive lures. In my experience, at least, the opposite is actually true of topwater bass bugs. Sometimes, in fact, I like to show the fish something that looks dramatically different from their prevalent species of prey, on the theory that it will get their attention quicker than a bug that looks like just one more of everything else in the water.

On the other hand, bass rarely pass up any hapless frog, kicking grasshopper, or half-dead shiner they find twitching on the surface. If you get a special kick out of "fooling" fish into thinking they're eating the real thing, by all means tie on an imitative bug. The bass won't object.

BASS BUG VARIETIES

Bass bugs are constructed from any lightweight material that floats: Cork, balsa, soft and hard foam, and spun deer hair are the most common. For all practical purposes, there are just two types: hard-bodied (cork, balsa, hard foam, plastic) and soft-bodied (deer hair and soft foam). Each type has some advantages and disadvantages.

A soft bug probably feels more natural and lifelike to a bass when he clomps down on it, so he's less

Frogs can be imitated in many ways. Both hard- and soft-bodied bugs can be deadly.

likely to spit it out instantly. It can be manipulated to gurgle and chug, or it can be twitched and slithered, flirted and fluttered in a variety of ways. Soft-bodied bugs can be dropped softly or splatted onto the water.

Hard bugs, of course, never get waterlogged, and, if they're well made, they'll last forever.

You don't need a steamer trunk full of bass bugs to be prepared for every occasion. If you carry just half a dozen bugs with you, you can usually stimulate a hungry bass's conditioned predatory response.

- *Popper.* The most versatile bug has a flat face, a tapered body, and a streamlined tail. It imitates nothing in particular and everything in general. All irrelevant decorations have been eliminated. I casts like a bullet and produces a variety of seductive noises when retrieved, which is everything you want.

Give it a slow tug to make it burble irresistibly. A harder, quicker pull makes it pop. Cast it against a fallen tree, along the edge of a weedbed, or against a rock, make it go *ploop,* and let it sit until the rings disappear. Give it a couple of little tugs. Rest it again. Keep it right there in the strike zone. Imagine the big bass that has come over for a look-see. Give it a twitch.

A popper with a wide, flat face that makes a big ruckus is your best choice for riffled or discolored water and at night, when bass hunt by sound rather than sight. Cup-faced bugs make an even louder pop than those with flat faces, but they tend to dig into the water when you pick them up to recast.

• *Slider.* On clear, flat, shallow water, a noisy popper might frighten bass. Here your best choice is a bug that slithers and undulates quietly. A slider such as a Feathered Minnow or a Sneaky Pete is one of the oldest floating bass lures, and it's still deadly. It has a small, bullet-shaped head and a long, wiggly tail. The slider rides low on the surface and gets its action from the creative manipulation of the angler.

Whether bass take the slider for a wounded baitfish is arguable, but it's certain that the same instinct that impels them to eat crippled minnows,

The Feathered Minnow slider is one of the oldest types of bass bugs.

worms, lizards, and any other unfortunate long, skinny creature that finds itself struggling on or near the water's surface prompts them to strike sliders.

A slider is a good choice when you want to cover a lot of water. Cast it among the reeds or over a sunken weedbed or a rocky point. Keep it moving at a steady but irregular pace and vary the speed until the bass tell you that you've got it right.

- *Deerhair Mouse.* I call it a mouse because to me it looks like a mouse. I'm not sure bass see it that way. Bass rarely pass up the chance to grab the unfortunate mouse or mole that finds itself on the water. Such opportunities, however, are rare.

don't show them a mouse to imitate what they're eating but simply to tempt them with an easy-to-catch and nourishing bellyful.

When bass see a mouse "bug," they see a lure that splits the difference between a popper and a slider. It won't pop, but it will burble and gurgle when you twitch it, and it will slither and slide and leave a wake of bubbles if you retrieve it slowly. The wiggly little whiskers and the long, sinuous tail are irresistible.

Try a mouse toward nightfall. Throw it right against the bank. Make it plop onto the water the way an unfortunate terrestrial creature accidentally falls in. Let it sit. It's momentarily stunned.

Mouse imitations featuring long slithery tails are extremely effective.

Now bring it to life. It's disoriented. It's panicky. It twitches, swims, pauses—the bass that swallows it in an implosion of water may not know it's supposed to be a mouse, but he's absolutely convinced it's good to eat.

- *Diver.* Larry Dahlberg designed this unique deer-hair bug that works both on and under the surface. The flat bottom, pointed nose, and high collar cause the diver to dart underwater when you give it a tug, while the long, sinuous tail gives it plenty of seductive action. The faster you retrieve it, the deeper it goes. Pause, and it bobs back to the surface. This up-and-down swimming motion mimics that of frogs and several other species of bass prey.

The Dahlberg Diver darts under the surface on the retrieve.

Use a Dahlberg Diver when sunlight or riffled water seems to discourage bass from coming to the surface. The diver also brings up bass when they're lying in deeper water. On a sinking line, the diver can be fished deep and made to hop along near the bottom, a happy option for those times when bass simply refuse to come to the top to eat.

- *Big Bug.* The theory is, "For big fish, use big lures." The theory seems to work, especially for largemouths. Nick Lyons introduced me to the specialized fun of hunting for the biggest bass in the pond with outsized deer-hair bugs tied on 4/0 and larger hooks. Any design will work, provided it offers a big silhouette, has legs and a tail to exaggerate the illusion of size, and makes plenty of noise when you give it a tug. Small bass might flee in terror, but every potbellied old lunker in the neighborhood will come over for a look.

Tie on a big bug at dusk and after dark, when the water goes flat and the cautious old big boys begin marauding in the shallow water. Cast it near likely cover, let it sit, make it go *glug* and *ker-ploop,* rest it again—and hold on.

If your big bug doesn't have terrible aerodynamics, it's not big and bulky enough. It takes a 10- or even a 12-weight rod to throw a big bug and a sturdy (6-foot, 20-pound) leader to turn it over. Of course, you'll need a sturdy outfit to subdue the bass that might inhale it.

This hefty smallmouth took a big deer-hair popper, proving the theory that big bugs take big fish. Credit: Will Ryan

- *Bluegill Bug.* Many anglers believe that no hungry bass will pass up an easy meal, regardless of how small it is. I'm convinced that there are times when bass of all sizes, particularly smallmouths, actually prefer something dainty and inoffensive.

  I don't hesitate to try a little generic foam- or cork-bodied bluegill bug with wiggly rubber legs whenever my full-sized bugs aren't doing the job. Sometimes the minibug turns the trick, and even if it doesn't, it casts like a dream on a trout-weight outfit. Bluegill bugs on Size 8 or 10 hooks are just right for the panfish that you always find in bass ponds, without being too small for bass. I tie one on whenever I just want a relaxing afternoon of no-pressure fishing, and I'm content to catch whatever wants to eat.

An assortment of panfish-sized bugs featuring wiggly rubber legs.

CHAPTER THREE

BASS UNDER THE SURFACE

Although bass are usually eager to slurp deer-hair and cork-bodied bugs off the top of the water, they're conditioned to find most of their food under the surface. So when conditions for bass-bug fishing are poor, or if you want to give yourself a slightly better chance of catching bass regardless of the conditions, a subsurface fly is your best choice.

Most commercial subsurface bass flies, like commercial bass bugs, are designed to imitate some form of natural prey—baitfish, leeches, crayfish, salamanders, or nymphs. Some flies are remarkably imitative, and others are vaguely suggestive. It's no more important for the angler to imitate a particular species of bass prey with subsurface flies than it is with bugs. Bass are opportunists. The creatures they encounter in the water make a bass buffet, and they eat whatever they can catch. Most of the time you can tie on a time-tested Woolly Bugger and be confident that you've got a fish-catcher on the end of your leader.

There are exceptions to this rule, especially with smallmouths. I have on occasion found them so keyed in on crayfish that only a fly that resembled and acted like a crayfish would catch them. When mayflies are hatching on a smallmouth river, the fish can be as selective as trout. In some Northeastern rivers, smallmouths feed almost exclusively on hellgrammites, a

36

nymph the size of a grown man's thumb, and only a fly that resembles a hellgrammite will catch them.

Experience—and reliable local sources—will tell you when to expect any of these exceptions. Otherwise, frankly, your choice of which fly to tie on is far less important than where you cast it and how you manipulate it in the water.

SUBSURFACE BASS FLY CHARACTERISTICS

Here are the characteristics to consider when selecting a subsurface fly:

- *Color.* In clear, shallow water under bright sun, go with a light-colored fly. Combinations of white, cream, tan, and yellow are good choices. Minimize the amount of flashy material in the fly. In bright sunlight, anything more than a hint of glitter is more likely to spook bass than to attract them.

  In clear water under cloud cover, use the same light colors, but go with a bit more flash.

  In murky water, darker colors such as black, purple, and dark olive work better. A hint of flash helps.

  Under almost any conditions, you can't go wrong with combinations of yellow and red, red and white, and green and white.

- *Size.* The old adage, "Big flies for big fish," generally holds true. For most conditions, a streamer 4 or 5 inches long on a 1/0 hook is a good choice

Old-fashioned bucktails in attention-getting colors still fool bass. Big eyes are added attractants.

for largemouths, and something 2 or 3 inches long on a Size 2 hook works best for smallmouths.

When the fishing is slow and you wouldn't mind catching a few perch, crappies, or bluegills while still having a chance for a bass, tie on a 1- or 2-inch streamer tied on a Size 6 or 8 hook. Bass eat a lot of small baitfish. At the other end of the spectrum, if you want to go big-game hunting for lunker bass and maybe a big northern pike or pickerel, and you're willing to get snubbed by small bass, tie on a big saltwater streamer. What you add in bulk, of course, you subtract in casting pleasure.

• *Decorations.* Baitfish, the No. 1 bass forage in most waters, have prominent eyes, and many experts believe that predatory fish focus on the eyes of their victims. Glued or painted eyes on streamers help trigger strikes.

Panicky baitfish flare their gills, which excites the predatory instinct of bass. A touch of red at the throat or behind the eyes of a streamer always helps.

- *Action.* The action of a fly—that is, how it moves in the water—should be lifelike to trigger the strike of a bass. Flies made from soft materials such as marabou, hackle feathers, wound hackles, and bucktail breathe and flare in the water. Rabbit strips wiggle and undulate. One of the great advantages fly fishermen enjoy over those who throw hardware

Variations on the old favorite, a yellow-and-red Mickey Finn bucktail. A touch of red at the throat helps imitate the flare of a baitfish's gills.

with spinning rods is the ability to present soft lures that appear lifelike and appetizing to hungry bass.

- *Weight.* Even small beadhead or dumbbell eyes on a sinking fly make casting difficult and tiring, but a little weight gets a subsurface fly down a foot or two where bass won't have to expose themselves near the surface to eat it. Weight near the front of the fly enhances its action in the water, too. It's a tradeoff.

  When you're not finding bass in the shallows— that is, in water less than 5 feet deep—your best bet, if you stick with a floating line, is a fly with enough weight to sink it down to where the fish are. If you decide your only alternative is to go deep, switch to a sinking or sink-tip line. For me, a heavily weighted fly or a sinking line is always a reluctant last resort, because casting them on a fly rod is simply no fun, and fishing blindly in deep water is, frankly, boring. Sometimes, however, it's the only chance to catch fish, and when the choice is fishing or quitting, I vote for fishing.

  Coneheads, dumbbell eyes, lead-wrapped bodies, and beadheads make any fly plummet toward the bottom. When they're retrieved with a series of tugs and pauses, they jig up and down in the water in an enticing manner. Let your weighted fly sink close to the bottom before beginning your retrieve, and then twitch it over the rocks and rubble where bass look for food. Over deep-water structure such as sunken weedbeds or brush piles, count down before you begin your retrieve, and

Sometimes bass ignore everything except crawfish imitations. Bead eyes help attract fish.

keep experimenting until the fish tell you you've found their depth. If you can put weighted flies near bass, they are deadly.

- *Weedguards.* A monofilament loop around the bend of the hook prevents snagging in weedy water and allows flies to crawl over stumps, tree branches, and rocks without hooking up. There's no reason not to arm all your bass flies with weedguards.

IMITATING BASS PREY

Bass are rarely finicky about what they eat. Drop an appetizing fly near them, make it move seductively, and they'll usually devour it, whether or not it happens to resemble the particular critter they ate most recently.

Time-proven bass attractors such as Mickey Finn bucktails, red-and-white streamers, Woolly Buggers, Clouser Minnows, and bunny flies continue to work most of the time. Maybe these flies look like something the fish recognize, but it's more likely that their action and color are what seduce bass into striking.

Nevertheless, it does no harm, and sometimes it does a lot of good, to tie on subsurface flies that at least suggest a species of prey that is commonly found in the water you are fishing. The movement you give your fly should likewise imitate that of the natural prey.

- *Baitfish.* All bass feed on other fish, including shiners, minnows, sculpins, sunfish, and baby bass. Baitfish imitations with eyes and gills, therefore, are always productive, and the well-

Bucktails in combinations of red and white are always deadly.

equipped bass angler will carry an assortment of bucktails and other streamers in a variety of colors and sizes. Experiment with the speed and cadence of your retrieve until you hit upon the one that catches fish. Sometimes bass want a series of fast, hard strips; other times you'll need to slow it down to a slow twitch . . . pause . . . twitch.

- *Leeches.* We called leeches "bloodsuckers" when I was a kid. These wormlike critters ranging from about 2 to 4 inches long are abundant in most lakes, ponds, and rivers. Bunny flies, Woolly Buggers, and marabou streamers in olive, tan, black, purple, and orange imitate leeches. Extra-long leech flies up to 7 inches long may not imitate the actual leeches that live in bass water, but they of-

Woolly Buggers work anywhere, anytime.

ten bring strikes from otherwise lock-jawed bass. Leeches swim slowly in an undulating motion, so a steady tug-pause-tug retrieve works best.

- *Crayfish.* In waters where crayfish are found, primarily cool, rocky smallmouth lakes and rivers, bass eat them voraciously. Woolly Buggers usually do the job, but closer imitations in tan and pale olive sometimes do it better. Crayfish crawl around on the bottom except when they're frightened. Then they move in a series of quick darts. In general, a very slow retrieve works best for crayfish flies.

- *Nymphs.* In cold-running smallmouth rivers, hellgrammites, caddis pupae, and mayfly and stonefly nymphs are important bass foods. These nymphs range in size from $\frac{1}{2}$ to nearly 2 inches long. Turn over a few rocks to see what's crawling underneath. That will help you decide what to tie on. Precise imitation is unimportant, but when you fish a river, carry an assortment of dark-colored (black, olive, and brown) buggy nymphs in sizes ranging from 12 to 4. Woolly Worms—or Woolly Buggers with the tails cut short—make excellent generic nymphs. Nymphs for moving water should be weighted and fished with a dead drift right along the bottom.

In ponds and lakes in the early summer, bass gluttonize on the inch-long nymphs of damselflies and dragonflies as they swim toward the shore where they will hatch into adults. Again,

Woolly Buggers and Woolly Worms do an acceptable job of suggesting these creatures, although closer imitations sometimes catch more fish. Still-water nymphs should be unweighted. Retrieve them like streamers with irregular twitches and tugs.

A FEW GOOD FLIES

You don't need hundreds of subsurface flies to be prepared for all situations. Here are seven designs that you can tie on with confidence any time. They're all a bass fisherman will ever need:

- *Woolly Bugger.* The Bugger, in a reasonable assortment of sizes and colors, may be the only underwater bass fly you'll ever need. It is a sugges-

Bass find long, slithery bunny flies irresistible.

tive imitation of virtually all bass prey, although I suspect its flaring hackle and wiggly marabou tail simply seduce bass regardless of what it might imitate. Supply tan, olive, and black Woolly Buggers in Sizes 6, 2, and 2/0, some with a beadhead, some unweighted.

- *Mickey Finn bucktail.* The combination of yellow and red and the lifelike look of bucktail in the water have been catching bass for decades. A 6-inch Mickey Finn is the best pike and pickerel fly I know.
- *Bunny fly.* This is simply a strip of rabbit fur and skin lashed to a hook. In olive, black, and brown, it makes a deadly leech imitation, although its

Slender Clouser Minnows with lead eyes work best when bumped along the bottom of a smallmouth river.

wiggly movement in the water unquestionably seduces bass regardless of what they take it for.

- *Muddler Minnow.* This old favorite resembles all manner of stubby bass prey, such as sculpins and tadpoles.
- *Woolly Worm.* Woolly Worms are as versatile as buggers. Worms can be twitched through the water to imitate baitfish, leeches, and damselfly nymphs, or they can be dead-drifted in moving water to imitate buggy stonefly nymphs and hellgrammites. Carry a few olive, brown, and black worms in Sizes 4 and 8, some with a little beadhead up front, and you'll be well armed.
- *Clouser Minnow.* The slim Clouser bucktail with its dumbbell eyes plummets to the bottom and rides upside down to minimize its chance of snagging. It's especially deadly in smallmouth rivers, but it works anytime you need to get deep.

In the final analysis, regardless of what you choose to tie to your leader, it's your ability to pick likely targets, cast the fly accurately, and manipulate it convincingly that will draw strikes.

CHAPTER FOUR

RIGGING UP

W hen I began bass fishing with my father, we used split-cane bamboo rods and silk lines. The rods were heavy, soft, and clunky. The taper of a fly line was designated by mysterious letters—HDH, for example, signified a double-tapered line—and matching it to a rod involved guesswork and trial and error. Those silk lines needed to be dried and greased up several times in an afternoon, because silk tended to sink. When a day's fishing ended, we stripped our line off the reel into loose coils on a newspaper to dry or else it would rot. The coating on those old silk lines tended to crack and otherwise deteriorate. If we left it on the reel over the winter, it would become kinky and tacky and useless.

I doubt if I could cast a big streamer or a bass bug very efficiently on one of those old 1950s outfits today, at least by my present-day standards, but I could back then—or at least it seemed to me that I could.

It should be clear by now that you can catch bass on almost any object with a hook in it. Put it in the water near a fish, give it a few twitches, and sooner or later some bass will try to eat it.

The same principle applies to the other components of your bass-fishing outfit. You can get a fly onto the water with any rig. With a poorly designed and unbalanced outfit, you'll be able to cast only short distances and with poor accuracy, and you will find it hard, exhausting work. If it enables you to drop a bug or a streamer near a bass, however, he won't care how it got there.

Fly-rod bass fishing involves more-or-less continuous casting. With a poorly matched or undersized outfit, it's hard work and not much fun. But modern floating fly lines, tapered and weighted to handle a bass fly and strung on a lightweight but powerful graphite rod designed for that size line, make casting bulky flies seem as natural as throwing a ball. With a well-balanced outfit, fly casting is intuitive, easy, and fun.

Visit any fly shop or call a reputable mail-order company, ask for an 8-weight bass-bugging outfit, and

For most fly-rod bass fishing, you only need a floating line. But at times, a sinking-tip line is necessary to take your fly down to the fish.

you can't go wrong. You'll end up with a weight-forward (forward-tapered, or "bass-bug" tapered), 8-weight, floating line (designated WF-8-F), a rod built to cast that line, and a reel for storing the line. Nowadays, gearing up can be just that easy.

Hand-picking an outfit that matches your physique and casting style is a better strategy, though, and the only way to do that is to cast the outfit before you buy it. Most fly shops will encourage you to try a rod on their casting pond or in their parking lot, and they'll be sure to put a sweet outfit in your hands. If you're a beginner, the clerk might give you a few gentle casting pointers. He'll want you to find it pleasant and easy, because then you'll be likely to make a purchase. Be sure to try it with a big bass fly or bug (cut off at the bend of the hook) tied to the leader. That's the only way to tell for sure if the outfit will serve your specific casting purpose.

You can get a complete outfit for around $200. It will do the job, and do it better than the most expensive equipment available fifty years ago.

Fly-fishing gear for bass is like most things: You get what you pay for, and expensive equipment generally (but not universally) works better than cheap stuff. If your budget is limited (whose isn't?), splurge on the rod and line, your casting tools, and skimp on the reel. If you want "the best" and appreciate fine workmanship, expensive components, and eye-catching aesthetics, you can invest a lot of money in fly-fishing gear and consider it well spent. Just understand that you might be paying for features that are irrelevant to how well the outfit actually casts a bass fly. Here's a more extensive analysis of the components of a bass fisherman's fly-fishing equipment.

THE LINE

The term "fly casting" is, technically, misleading. Fly casting really involves casting a line which happens to have a fly attached to the end of it. You can fly cast without a fly and barely notice the difference. When you select an outfit for most kinds of fly fishing, you first choose a suitable line and then select a rod that will cast that line efficiently.

Because even streamlined bass flies, and especially floating bugs, are heavy and air-resistant compared to tiny trout flies, smooth, easy casting calls for a slick line with enough density to compensate for the bulk of the fly. A 7- or 8-weight line (which, if you care, means a line of which the first 30 feet weigh anywhere from 177 to 218 grains) will handle all but the most outrageously air-resistant bass flies with ease. If you fish exclusively with small, streamlined bugs and unweighted subsurface flies, you can cast comfortably with a 5- or 6-weight outfit. If you like to use big bugs or heavily weighted flies, you'll need a 9- or 10-weight rig.

A weight-forward line enables you to throw a bass fly with a minimum of false casting. The "bass-bug" taper puts even more weight up at the front of the line than the standard weight-forward taper, and makes smooth, accurate casting that much easier.

Ninety percent of fly-rod bassing is best done with a floating line. A floating line enables you to manipulate a bug or streamer easily and lift the line off the water to begin your next cast more efficiently than you could with a sinking line.

In practice, even a "floating" line might begin to sink after an hour of fishing. This happens when the microscopic aquatic growth and other crud that scums the surface of nutrient-rich bass water accumulates on the line. Carry a square of felt impregnated with line cleaner with you (if yours is not a Wonderline) along with a dry rag, and whenever your line begins to sink, take a few minutes to dry and clean it. Simply running most lines, especially Wonderlines, through a dry rag while pinching it tight against the line will remove most of the algae and keep it afloat.

When you don't find bass in shallow water, you'll want to explore the deeper water around dropoffs, points, and underwater rock piles. Then a sinking-tip weight-forward line will help take your fly down to the fish.

Lines come in colors ranging from neon green, yellow, orange, and red to neutral shades of gray and brown. There is no evidence that bright-colored floating lines spook bass (although the shadow or flash of a line in the sun over a bass's head *will* spook him). Choose a line that's highly visible to you. On dark days, in twilight, and in shadows, a bright-colored line enables you to locate a floating bug quickly.

High-quality fly lines are worth the extra few dollars they cost. They float better and come with slicker, more durable finishes than budget-priced lines. In the long run, a top-grade line lasts longer, casts smoother, and is a sounder investment than a cheap line.

THE LEADER

Bass are not normally leader-shy. The main job of the bass leader is to continue the line's taper, giving you something thin enough at its end to poke through the eye of a hook and tie into a solid knot. A smoothly tapered line and leader combination won't collapse on itself or otherwise mess up your casting. For most purposes, a tapered leader between 7 and 9 feet long, including tippet, that tests at 8 to 12 pounds, will handle all the bass flies you'll want to cast and all the bass you're likely to hook. Leaders of this size, which are

"Big-game" leaders and a few spools of tippet material will easily last an entire season.

generally sold as "saltwater leaders," are perfect. To turn over very large bugs and streamers, or to horse bass out of thick weeds, use a leader that tests at 15, or even 20, pounds. The extra .001 or .002 inch in diameter will not scare off a bass that wants to eat your fly.

A good leader should be on the stiff side, with a hard finish. The butt end should be about the same diameter as the end of your fly line for a smooth continuing taper. Leaders come in a variety of more-or-less transparent colors, but there is no evidence that bass care.

Start with a knotless tapered leader 7½ feet long that tests at 12 pounds. This is sturdy enough to turn over all but the bulkiest flies. After changing flies a few times and throwing a wind knot or two into the end of it, just cut it back and add 15 to 20 inches of 12-pound-test tippet. This way, you should be able to get through a whole season without having to replace the leader itself.

Knotted leaders tend to pick up weeds and gunk at the knots, a problem that knotless tapered leaders prevent.

THE ROD

The fly rod should match the line. The weight designation of a rod (for example, an 8-weight rod) simply refers to the line it's designed to cast and has nothing to do with the actual weight of the rod.

You can cast bass flies with bamboo or fiberglass rods, but nowadays graphite is a far superior fly-rod material. Bass fishing involves a lot of casting. A good graphite rod makes the difference between casting pleasure and casting agony.

Today's graphite fly rods come in a bewildering variety of sizes, flexes, designs, and prices. Selecting the "right" one can feel like a major project, but it's worth the time and effort. Some rods "track" better than others and are inherently more accurate. This quality is generally reflected in the rod's price. If a rod consistently throws curves in your line and lands your fly to one side or the other of where you aim, or if you feel that you're laboring to cast 50 feet, it doesn't matter whether the flaw lies in the rod or in your casting style. Discard that rod and try another.

The way a rod flexes should suit your casting style. Contemporary rod makers use a variety of terminologies to indicate how a rod bends—"fast," "medium," and "slow," for example, or "tip-flex," "mid-flex," and "full-flex." Because bass flies, especially bugs, are inherently air-resistant, a "medium" or "mid-flex" rod works best for most anglers.

The most expensive fly rods come with pretty wrappings, fancy reel seats, and top-quality hardware. Many low-end rods come with cheap hardware and plain wrappings but are made from the same blanks, and, therefore, perform as well as the pricier ones produced by the same manufacturer.

A good bass rod is long enough to keep your backcast off the water when you're sitting in a canoe, wading up to your waist, or drifting in a float tube. A rod at least 9 feet long enables you to lift a lot of line off the water to begin your backcast and gives you added leverage when you're fighting a fish.

The best all-round bass rod, then, is a 9-foot, 8-weight mid-flex graphite that you can cast comfortably. The pleasure it brings you will be worth whatever you pay for it.

THE REEL

Expensive reels offer definite advantages for some kinds of fishing. Whenever you expect to encounter hard-running fish such as salmon, big trout, and almost all saltwater species, a reel with a smooth, reliable disc drag that holds a couple hundred yards of backing can make the difference between catching and losing hooked fish.

For bass fishing, however, the reel serves primarily as a line-storing device. Bass do not run hard, fast, or for long distances. I have never hooked a bass that peeled the entire length of my line off the reel and took me into my backing (though I'm looking forward to the first time). Bass will bore for cover when they're hooked. They're strong and dogged fighters, but they're sloggers and jumpers, not high-speed long-distance sprinters. The rod, not the reel, is your bass-fighting tool.

If you want to save money on your bass outfit, economize with an inexpensive reel. Just be sure it's big enough to store the line and at least 100 feet of backing (just in case).

THE FLY BOX

I own hundreds of bass flies, but a good afternoon of bass fishing does not require a large assortment of

Keep streamers in a transparent fly box with large compartments.

Don't cram too many bugs in your fly box. A couple of each type are all you need to have with you.

flies. When I go fishing, I only bring two boxes with me. One holds perhaps fifteen bugs—no more than fit comfortably in a single container. The other holds an assortment of subsurface flies. For river smallmouths, I add a small box of dry flies and nymphs.

You can dump a few flies in a plastic bag and catch as many fish. But a large plastic fly box works better. Pick one with a securely locking lid and compartments that are large enough to prevent your flies from getting bent and squashed. Drill a few small air holes in the bottom of your fly box so that the moisture from the damp flies you put back can escape and the hooks won't rust.

SUNGLASSES

You should *not* try to economize on sunglasses. High-quality glasses are at least as important to your fishing pleasure as your fly rod. Good sunglasses protect your eyes from dangerous ultraviolet rays, cut surface glare, deflect stray hooks, keep wind and airborne particles from blowing into your eyes, prevent headaches, and enable you to spot fish and study the bottom through the water's surface. Wearing poor glasses is worse than wearing no glasses at all.

The best sunglasses are made from ophthalmic glass, which is distortion-free and scratch-resistant. They provide 100-percent ultraviolet (UV) protection and zero distortion. Fishing glasses should have polarized lenses to cut glare. Amber is the best all-round color.

Mandatory sun protection: wide-brimmed hat, polarized sunglasses, and sunblock.

Aside from the fact that you can pay extra for style and brand name, it's fairly safe to say that with sunglasses, you get what you pay for.

CLOTHING

Your mother has already taught you to dress warmly when it's cold outside and to wear raingear when it's wet. Clothing should also provide protection from the sun. Loosely woven fabrics such as T-shirts do not filter out UV radiation, thereby heightening your risk of skin cancer. When fishing in the sun, wear long-sleeved shirts made from tightly woven fabrics, and don't forget to slather on the sunblock.

This angler is dressed just right for bass fishing. Credit: Art Scheck

Everything you wear should be in neutral colors such as beige, gray, or olive, especially if you're wading. Bright colors like yellow, pink, and white catch the attention of fish and frighten them.

Your baseball cap shades your eyes and forehead but does not shield your lower face, nose, ears, or neck from the sun. For best protection from the sun, wear a hat with a solid (not mesh) 4-inch brim all around.

OTHER IMPORTANT STUFF

When you want to prowl or wade along the shoreline of a bass pond or creek, travel light. You should be able to carry everything you need in your shirt pockets or a fanny pack. In a rowboat or canoe, stow it all in a waterproof canvas bag. In addition to rod, reel, and fly box, the well-equipped bass fisherman will bring:

- *Landing net.* Although not really a necessity (hand-landing bass is easy), when you're fishing from a boat a long-handled, wide net is the best way to land, unhook, and release bass without harming them.
- Spools of 8-, 10-, and 12-pound-test *tippet material.*
- *Needle-nosed pliers* for mashing down the barbs of hooks.
- *Forceps* for unhooking deeply hooked fish.
- *Scissors* for cutting leaders and reshaping flies.
- A tube of SPF-30 broad-spectrum *sunscreen.* Lather it onto all exposed skin first thing and reapply it every couple of hours.
- *Fly flotant.* Thick liquid flotant, fingered into deer-hair bugs, keeps them buoyant for hours.

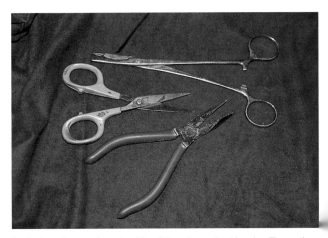

Tools: long forceps for unhooking fish, scissors for trimming flies and cutting leader, and needle-nosed pliers for debarbing hooks and a myriad of other jobs.

- *Line cleaner.* Carry a square of felt impregnated with line cleaner in a small plastic bag, and use it every couple of hours.
- *Flashlights.* If you expect to be out after dark, which might occur any time you set forth in the afternoon, carry two lights: a small, narrow-focus one for knot tying, and a stronger one for lighting your way off the water and when packing away your gear.

   Several useful knot-tying lights are available that are designed to leave both hands free. There are lights you can clench in your teeth, lights that attach to the bill of your cap, lights that clip onto the front of your shirt, and even lights that clinc around your thumb. Pick one that works for you, and be sure not to shine it on the water. Sudden flashes of light at night can spook bass.

When you're unloading your gear and walking through the woods at night, a headlamp always aims in the right direction and keeps both hands free for more important chores like lugging and loading gear and pushing aside brush.

- *Insect repellent.*
- A plastic bottle for *drinking water.*

KNOTS

Many fishermen pride themselves on their knot-tying prowess and can show you how to make dozens of interesting and complicated knots. When you're sitting in a boat in failing light with mosquitoes swarming around your face and big bass sloshing near the bank, however, you're best off if you can tie just a few simple, dependable knots quickly and automatically.

There are many excellent handbooks on knots. Follow the diagrams and practice tying the few that you'll need so that when you're on the water, you won't have to think about what you're doing. Lubricate all knots with saliva, be sure to pull them tight, leave short whiskers when you clip the ends, and test them by pulling hard on them. There's nothing more disheartening than losing a big fish because you tied a careless knot.

When you're actually out fishing, you'll rarely need more than two knots, one for tying the fly to the tippet and one for tying the tippet to the leader.

Tying a Trilene Knot (modified Clinch Knot—twice through the eye)

1. Start this knot the same way as you would start a Clinch Knot, but after you have brought the tippet through the hook eye, keep coming around and pass the tippet through the hook eye a second time, in the same direction as the first pass. This will form a double loop in front of the eye as you start to make your turns around the standing part of the line. Keep this loop open with the thumb and forefinger of your left hand.

2. Wind the tag end around the standing part *five times only*. Bring the tag end back through the double loop in front of the eye.

3. Moisten and tighten carefully. Instead of letting go of the tag end as you would when tightening a Clinch Knot, it helps to hold the tag end tightly against the fly.

These are the two knots I use when I'm out bass fishing. They are easy to learn and quick to tie, and I've never had a failure with either of them.

- *Trilene Knot.* This is such an efficient and easy-to-make knot that I use it exclusively to tie my bass flies to my tippet. The Trilene Knot is stronger than the popular modified Clinch Knot, which it resembles.

- *Surgeon's Knot.* The Surgeon's Knot is simply a double overhand knot used for joining tippet to leader. Properly tied, it's close to 100-percent efficient, which means it's as strong as the leader it's tied with. There is no evidence, by the way, that the Surgeon's Knot has ever actually been used in surgery.

Surgeon's Knot

1. Overlap the tag ends of the two strands you are joining by 4 to 6 inches. The section not attached to the rest of your leader and line (in most cases a new tippet) should start in your left hand.

2. Form a loop in the overlapped strand and pinch the junction of the loop with the thumb and forefinger of your right hand.

3. Using your left hand, wrap the standing part of the tippet (or smaller piece) and the tag end of the bigger piece through the loop three times. Treat them as a single piece; they'll stay together easier if you wet them with saliva. Many sources recommend using only two turns, but lab tests have shown us that the Triple Surgeon's Knot is marginally stronger and no harder to make with a third turn.

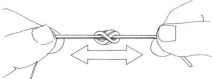

4. Tighten this knot by holding both short and long ends on each side and pulling quickly and tightly. Make sure all strands are snug, then trim the tag ends as close to the knot as possible.

There are two other knots that you should know. You'll rarely be called upon to tie them when you're actually out fishing, but you'll need them for gearing up.

- *Nail Knot.* Use a Nail Knot for joining the butt end of your leader to the end of your fly line. It's slim, neat little knot that slides smoothly through the rod's guides, and it doesn't "hinge" when casting the way loop-to-loop connections might. A piece of drinking straw or a fly-tying bobbin work better than a nail. Finish your nail knots with drop of strong, quick-drying waterproof glue, both to secure it and to give it a smooth finish.
- *Duncan Loop Knot.* For attaching backing to the arbor of your reel, this simple sliding clinch knot does the job.

Rather than knotting the leader to the line and the tippet to the leader, many anglers prefer loop-to-loop connections. Interlocked loops make changing leaders and tippets quick and easy.

Many fly-line makers provide a factory-made loop at the business end. Knot manuals give instructions for several methods of creating a permanent loop in your line. To attach the leader, tie a loop in the butt end and link the two loops. Tie a loop in the thin end of the leader and another in one end of the tippet, and you can change tippet a hundred times without shortening the leader.

The easiest, quickest, and strongest leader loop is the Double Surgeon's Loop. It's just two overhand knots.

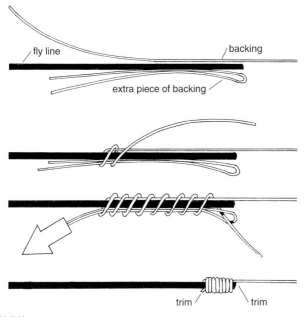

fly line

backing

extra piece of backing

trim   trim

Nail Knot

The Nail Knot can be tied in four steps (top to bottom).

1. To tie, make a loop and overlap the tag end with the standing part of the leader for about 5 inches. Pinch the material close to the top of the loop and near the bottom of the overlap.
2. Tie a loose overhand knot in the doubled section and pass the single loop through the double loop you have just formed. Don't tighten.
3. Make another turn of the single loop through the doubled loop. In other words, make a double overhand knot in the doubled section.
4. Moisten the knot. Tighten it by pulling the loop away from both the tag end and the standing part of the line. Make sure you pull equally on the standing part and the tag end of this knot, unlike the Perfection Loop. Trim the tag end closely.

CHAPTER FIVE

CASTING AND RETRIEVING

Shallow-water bass fishing is target-shooting—that is, identifying those pockets, alleys, and edges that look "bassy," dropping your streamer or bug right where you want to, and doing it again and again as you move slowly along a brush-strewn shoreline, a weedy cove, or a jumble of boulders. Picking your targets and hitting them consistently offers a continual series of challenges for the fly caster. It's lots of fun. It's also the key to catching bass on flies.

I was about twelve years old the first time my father invited me to go bass fishing with him. A year of trout fishing had taught me the rudiments of fly casting, and it didn't take me too long to get a feel for the heavier rod with the deer-hair popper Dad had tied to the end of my leader. I managed to plop the bug along the edges of the lily pads and near the pilings of the occasional boat dock we encountered along that shoreline, and I caught a few small bass.

When we came to an oak tree that grew at a low angle out over the water, Dad held the canoe. He didn't have to tell me that this was a particularly bassy spot.

I dropped the bug along the edge of the shadow cast by the overhanging boughs three or four times, with no strikes.

With a strong sidearm cast you can drive a bass fly under overhanging bushes.

"Cast it way under those branches," Dad said. "There's a big old bass hiding in that dark hole right against the bank."

"That's impossible," I said. "I'll snag the tree."

He shrugged.

I handed the rod to him.

"Show me," I said, quite confident that he couldn't.

Of course, he did. He made two false casts, and with a sidearm cast and a loop about a foot wide, he drove the bug way under the low branches and dropped it against the bank. One twitch, and a four-pound large-mouth engulfed it.

He fought the fish quickly, lip-landed it, unhooked the bug from the corner of its mouth, held it up for me to admire, and released it. Then he handed the rod back to me.

"Like that," he said.

It was a powerful lesson—four lessons, really—that still guide me fifty years later: Not all bass targets are easy to hit, but they're all worth hitting; the most difficult targets are often the ones that produce the biggest fish; bass won't move far to take a fly, so you've got to get it close to them; and, the angler who can cast accurately will have the best luck.

In other words, luck has very little to do with it.

The other key to catching bass on flies, which I absorbed from watching my father do it, is moving the fly on or through the water in an enticing manner once you hit the bull's-eye with it.

CASTING

Fishermen who are used to casting tiny trout flies on lightweight rods often find casting bass-sized flies awkward and laborious, at least at first. Even the smallest, lightest, and most streamlined bass flies are heavier and more air-resistant than most trout flies. Casting them efficiently and accurately requires the right equipment, sound technique, and practice.

- *Equipment.* Nobody can cast a bass fly efficiently if his fly line is too light to overcome the bulk of the fly, and if his rod doesn't match his line. No outfit is too heavy to handle a bass fly, but it can certainly be too light. The line-and-rod combination you need to move a big, bulky bug or sogg streamer through the air will also cast a small fly easily.

On the other hand, bass fishing is a continuous process of casting, retrieving, lifting line off the water, and casting again, interrupted now and then, we hope, by fighting a fish. Repeatedly moving a 9- or 10-weight line, with a big, bulky bass fly tied to the end of it, through the air will cause even a well-conditioned athlete's shoulder to ache. That's why I recommend using streamlined, medium-sized flies for most situations and reserving the oversized bugs for an hour or so at dusk, and the weighted flies and sink-tip lines for times when nothing else works.

- *Technique.* A 7- or 8-weight line with a bass bug or bass-sized streamer tied to the tippet, even on a well-matched rod, moves through the air more slowly than a thin trout-weight line. The tip-action rod and the quick, wristy casting stroke that combine to work well for false-casting and air-drying tiny dry flies spell disaster for bass bugging.

A medium-action rod and a slow, smooth casting stroke work together to give the heavy line with the bass fly on the end of it time to straighten out on the back- and forward cast. Keep your wrist stiff and use your entire arm and shoulder to move the rod. Resist the impulse to compensate by trying to overpower the weight of the line and the air-resistance of the fly or by speeding up your stroke. The best way to find the right timing is to watch your backcast unfurl over your shoulder.

Don't begin your forward stroke until you see that the line has straightened out behind you. Soon you'll learn to feel the line loading the rod, and you won't need to look.

An efficient, powerful casting stroke produces a minimal of false casting, tight casting loops, and pinpoint accuracy. It's all about line speed, and line speed comes from accelerating the rod on both the forward and the backcast and from stopping the rod abruptly when it reaches about one o'clock on the backcast and ten o'clock on the forward cast. Do this properly and you'll see how the rod, not the caster, does all the work.

You can achieve even greater line speed by mastering the single or double haul.

With the right outfit, a strong but smooth stroke, and the proper timing, you'll have no trouble casting a bass fly as far as you'll ever need to. Smooth, easy casting is just a matter of rhythm and letting the rod and line do their job. If you find yourself straining to reach bassy targets, move a little closer. There's rarely any reason to cast more than fifty feet.

Recognizing likely bass targets and hitting them consistently with a well-cast fly, more than any other factor, including the streamer or bug with which you choose to fish, are what separate successful bass anglers from everyone else. Accuracy which comes from line speed and tight loops, is more important than delicacy in bass fishing, so don't worry if your fly splats down on the water.

One of the advantages of flies over hardware is that even big, bulky flies hit the water with a natural-sounding, fish-attracting *plop*. Unless you drop it directly atop a basking bass, that *splat* is more likely to attract a nearby fish than spook him.

Fly casting is inherently more accurate than other methods of delivering a lure. A reasonably competent fly caster controls the distance and direction of his line throughout the cast. He can hit the bull's-eye more consistently than all but the elite bait- or spin-casters, which is one big advantage you as a fly caster have over those high-tech folks. False casting allows for fine-tuning distance and aim before dropping the fly onto the water, and you can pull back a cast before it hits the water if you realize it's destined to be off-target. Don't false cast excessively, however; the flash and shadow of a line in the air can spook a bass.

Bass usually hold tight to bankside logs, rocks, and weedbeds and under overhanging limbs, bushes, and docks. They do not normally like to move far from their cover to eat. If you want to entice them to devour your fly, you've got to put it close to them, so cast aggressively. If you don't occasionally overshoot your target, you're probably being too cautious.

Work on casting those hard, tight loops. By dropping your rod to a horizontal position, you can make a forceful sidearm cast that will cause a deer-hair bug to ricochet off the water's surface and skip under overhanging cover.

Another advantage you as a fly caster enjoy over your spinning and bait-casting counterparts is the ability to make another cast as soon as you've fished the productive water. There's rarely any need to retrieve a fly all the way to the boat. Work it through the good-looking water, usually no more than halfway back to you, then pick up your line and begin your next cast.

To start your next cast, don't try to get the fly airborne until most of your line is off the water. First, be sure that your rod is pointing at the fly and your line is straight. Then raise your rod smoothly and simultaneously pull back on the line with your line hand. This will load your rod, lift your line off the water before the fly, and start it moving into a smooth, strong backcast.

- *Practice.* To get the feel of your bassing outfit and to become a consistently accurate caster, you've got to practice. If you don't mind not catching many fish, of course, you can practice only when you're actually out fishing; but if you want to take advantage of your precious time on the water, get out in the yard or drive to the nearest playground with your bass outfit.

It's wise to use last year's fly line for practicing on grass or asphalt. The abrasion from casting on anything but water will quickly ruin the coating of a line. Cut the bend of the hook off a bug or streamer similar to one you might use on the water, tie it on, and practice casting.

For backyard practice, use the kind of fly you'll actually fish with, but cut off the bend. Credit: Vicki Stiefel

First, work on your technique. Don't go for distance. Bass fishing never demands long-distance casting. Measure out fifty feet on the lawn. That's as far as you'll ever need to cast a bass fly. Practice lifting your line smoothly. Work on your stroke and your timing. Go for consistently tight casting loops. Your goal should be to drive the fly fifty feet with no more than two false casts.

Then focus on your accuracy. The best way to do this is to replicate the actual bass-fishing challenges you're likely to encounter on the water. If you expect to be casting from the bow seat of a canoe or rowboat, for example, bring a stool or milk crate with you, sit on it so that you're at a right

To hone your accuracy in the backyard, cast to small targets such as pie plates. Include sidearm casts from a crouching position to replicate actual fishing situations. Credit: Vicki Stiefel

If you intend to fish from a boat or canoe, practice casting from a low sitting position. Credit: Vicki Stiefel

angle to your target as you would be when your watercraft is moving parallel to the shoreline, and practice casting across your body from a low sitting position. If you like to wade in knee-deep water, kneel when you practice casting. If you expect to be prowling a shoreline afoot, practice casting sidearm while squatting or hunching over.

With a little imagination, you can create a virtual shoreline in your backyard. Place a dozen aluminum pie plates in imaginary bass holes—alongside the trunk of your apple tree, beside your bird bath, under the branches of your rhododendron, against your stone wall, or perhaps on the edge of your flower garden. Move from target to target, and see how many casts it takes to hit each pie plate.

Keep score, if that appeals to you. Make a game of it, like golf. Give yourself out-of-bounds penalties for snagging branches. You can even compete with your fishing partner. When you master your "course," place your pie plates closer to the bushes or in narrower alleys and move back five feet from your targets to the "expert tees."

PUTTING THE FLY TO WORK

- *The Retrieve.* Old-time bass-bug fishermen were almost unanimous in their insistence that you couldn't retrieve a bug slowly enough. The common rule of thumb in those politically incorrect days was: After your bug hits the water, lay your rod across your lap, light a cigarette, and smoke the entire thing before giving the bug its first twitch. Nonsmokers ate sandwiches.

  The theory behind this approach depended on a conception of bass behavior that experience bears out only occasionally. Bass, according to the old-timers, needed to be teased into striking. They'd swim over to investigate whatever plopped onto the water, and then they'd lie there looking at it, waiting for it to make the first move, trying to decide if it was good to eat. If it just fell to the water and swam away, Mr. Bass would shrug and return to his lair.

  There is no question that the patient waiting game sometimes works. It's a lot easier to execute when your bug has landed beside a shady deadfall or in a pothole surrounded by lily pads where you just *know* a big bass is lurking. When you're working your way down a shoreline that features one likely target after the other, however, and a particularly bassy cove lies just around the next point, spending several minutes to fish out each cast requires superhuman will power; in the back of your mind, you suspect you might be wasting precious fishing time that could be better invested in that next hotspot.

Fifty years of bass fishing has given me no convincing evidence that leaving a bug motionless on the water for more than half a minute catches bass that wouldn't take it if it moved more quickly.

Say what you want about tournament bass fishermen; they know how to catch fish. Rarely do the pros use the super-slow retrieve with their floating lures. In fact, they generally just chuck it out and chug it back. They vary the speed and rhythm of their retrieve depending on the lure and, I'm sure, a vast array of other variables known only to them, but they do tend to keep the thing moving.

If eating a sandwich before giving their lure its first twitch would catch more bass, you can be sure that when prize money is on the line, the professional bass catchers would do it that way.

We tend to impute human characteristics to the fish we hunt. We believe they have "moods," that they can be "angered" into striking, that they are susceptible to "teasing" or "tormenting," or that they can be "stubborn" or "cautious." Maybe, maybe not. The fact is that most of the time, bass simply do what their instincts drive them to do to survive: They spawn when the urge is upon them, they seek shelter and comfortable water, they flee from danger—and they eat.

Natural bass foods don't all behave the same way, and there's no reason to think that the fish prefer one behavior over another. A grasshopper begins kicking desperately the instant it hits the water. A mouse begins swimming as soon as it splashes down. A moth flutters its wings for a moment before lying still. A frog swims, pauses to look around, then swims some more. An injured or disoriented baitfish churns around the surface. Nearby bass will devour any one of these bits of nourishment with equal enthusiasm.

The message for the bass fisherman is this: By all means, vary the speed and cadence of your retrieve, whether you're casting a floater or a subsurface fly, but don't waste a lot of time fishing over water that might be barren. If they don't strike on the first couple of casts, they're either not there, or they're not hungry.

I have caught a lot of bass, especially, for some reason, smallmouths, by beginning my retrieve as soon as my fly hits the water and keeping it coming steadily back in a series of forceful twitches and jerks, which Dave Whitlock calls the "panic strip." It works especially well over deep-water bass cover such as reefs, sunken weedbeds, and drowned timber, where you need to grab and hold the attention of fish that have to swim up from the bottom to strike. I have also found the panic strip effective when casting to bass during their spawning season.

One of the advantages of bass bugs is the variety of noises and movements you can impart to them, all the way from subtle vibrations to loud, attention-grabbing pops. Leave it motionless, vibrate it, and let it lie. Make it go *glug* and *kerploop.* Try a twitch-pause-twitch retrieve, or vary it by alternating a hard panic strip with a pause. Mix and match. Try them all.

The same principle applies to subsurface flies. Vary the speed and the cadence of the retrieve until the bass tell you what they like best.

Some days one method seems to work better than others, but I suspect that most of the time, it makes less difference than many experts claim. A hungry bass will eat. If he's not hungry, it may take more than a tantalizing fly to change his mind. Yes, you might be able to anger or otherwise persuade him into striking, and if you're convinced he's there and he's a big one, it's worth trying. In that case, the fast, steady retrieve is just as likely to induce him to inhale your fly as that agonizingly slow twitch-pause-twitch.

- *The straight line.* Regardless of the kind of movement you give your fly or the speed of your retrieve, always keep your rod tip low and pointing directly at the fly. Manipulate the fly by tugging on the line, not by twitching or jerking the rod itself. Maintaining a straight line down the rod, line and leader all the way to your fly, keeps you in control. A 1-inch tug on the line moves the fly 1 inch. Tug hard and it darts forward. Tug gently and it twitches, wiggles, and vibrates.

Moving the fly by lifting your rod or yanking it sideways creates slack in your line that leaves you out of control and could cost you a hookup. By keeping your rod tip low and the line straight, you are ready for a strike at all times. Should you get a hit but fail to hook up, the strip-strike leaves your fly right there where Mr. Bass can find it and, perhaps, try to eat it a second time.

When retrieving, keep your rod tip low and pointed at the fly. This lets you stay in complete control. Credit: Will Ryan

Use a stripping basket to prevent line tangles in a boat or when wading.
Credit: Will Ryan

- *Line management.* Be sure the bottom of the boat between your feet is clear of stray tackle, protruding nuts and bolts, your shoelaces, and all the other odds and ends that lie in wait to snag and tangle your stripped-in line and short-circuit your casts, always at the worst possible time. Float tubes generally come equipped with an apron that spreads across your lap to hold your line. When you're casting from the shore, wading in weedy or brushy water, and even casting from a boat, a stripping basket will prevent foulups and give you control of your loose line.

CHAPTER SIX

NAVIGATING

Y ou can stand on a boat dock and cast into the water for an entire afternoon, or until your arm goes limp, if you want. Once you've covered the water around you with a couple dozen casts, however, every bass within range will have seen your fly and decided whether he wants to eat it. Stay long enough, of course, and a few new bass may cruise into casting range.

Remaining stationary is an inefficient way to fish for bass. To maximize your chances of catching fish, you've got to cover a lot of water. There are two ways to move around: by floating and afoot.

FLOATING

You can fish for bass from anything that floats. Different watercraft offer the bass fisherman advantages and disadvantages, and your best choice depends on both the type of water you want to fish and your idea of fun.

- *Bass boats.* These are designed to get you there fast, and though their gadgets, mechanics, and electronics might strike you as incompatible with fly fishing, the "quiet sport," there is no denying their efficiency. In a sleek bass boat with a 50-horsepower motor, you can scoot from the north end of a good-sized lake or reservoir to the sheltered shoreline on the south end without wasting a lot of fishing time, and then, with its shallow draft and weedless electric motor, you can prowl coves and creep along the edges of weedbeds, steering with your foot to leave both hands free for casting while you perch high on a swiveling seat.

A fully equipped bass boat along with the trailer you need to get it to the water (not to mention the truck you need to pull the trailer) is by far your most expensive option.

The main practical disadvantage of bass boats (aside from their cost) is that they limit the number of places you can fish. You cannot slide a trailered boat into a pond, lake, or river that doesn't have a launch area where you can back your trailer into the water. Moreover, any place that offers launching facilities for you provides them for other fishermen as well. Be prepared to share the water or even compete for it.

- *A lightweight aluminum rowboat.* This craft, with a small (four- or five-horsepower) outboard on the transom and a pair of oars offers a more affordable and flexible option. You need a trailer to move it around, but once you get there, you don't need a public boat ramp to launch it. Two men can carry the boat to the water's edge. Aluminum rowboats aren't built for speed, but what's your hurry? You'll be fishing water that the bass-boat boys can't reach, so there's no need to race around to be there first.

Chug down to that bassy cove with the lily pads and fallen trees, turn off the motor, tilt it up, grab

A sturdy aluminum rowboat custom-designed for bass fishing, with a small outboard, an electric steering motor, and a swivel seat. Credit: John Likakis

the oars, and hand your partner the fly rod. In a stable, wide-bottomed rowboat, the fisherman can stand up to cast without capsizing. Once you've fished that water, crank up the motor and go looking for another place.

A rowboat with a small outboard offers the ideal way to drift a smallmouth river. Use the oars to keep the caster a comfortable casting distance from the shore, and let the current carry you along. When you're done for the day, you can relax and let the motor take you back.

- *Wooden rowboats.* These are relatively impractical bass-stalking craft. They're heavy, awkward, uncomfortable, and slow even with a motor mounted on the transom. They tend to leak, their oarlocks usually creak, and unless you keep it moored on your favorite pond or lake, you need a trailer to get it into the water, making all those lightly fished bass hotspots without launching facilities inaccessible.

   Still, my first memories of bass fishing are of taking turns at the oars with my father, and in my imagination, rowboats and bass go together like blueberry pancakes and Vermont maple syrup. Bass fishing and rowboats are both old-timey, leisurely, and low tech. Casting flies to a shoreline from a rowboat seems to tap into something utterly comfortable and evocative.

- *Canoes.* They are more portable than bass boats or rowboats. Even without a small outboard mounted on the transom of a square-ender, canoes are as

A canoe will take you to backwaters and unpressured fishing that are inaccessible to bigger boats.

swift as rowboats. With their shallow draft you can go just about anywhere in a canoe. A 13-foot aluminum canoe weighs about 45 pounds, light enough for a pair of intrepid bass fishermen, taking turns, to carry on their shoulders for a mile or more into remote, secret ponds. Canoes are ideal watercraft for two anglers who enjoy taking turns on a small body of water. They are less stable than rowboats, however, and trying to paddle and hold a position and cast a fly all at the same time is more than one man can comfortably handle.

- *One-man watercraft.* Solo craft, including kayaks, float tubes, kickboats, and pontoon boats, offer the bass fisherman the stealthiest approach and access to the greatest variety of waters. A one-man self-powered watercraft is the best way to get out alone and fish intimate bass water.

A float tube is an inflated truck-sized inner tube with a canvas covering, a sling seat, and an inflated backrest. Float tubes are manufactured with the fly fisherman in mind. They provide zippered pockets for fly boxes and other gear, and they come equipped with an apron to snap over your lap to hold your loose line. You wear swim fins, sit inside the tube with your butt in the water, and kick your feet to move.

Because you travel backward in a tube, the best strategy for right-handed casters is to travel counter-clockwise (clockwise, of course, for a left-handed caster) along a shoreline or around a

oat tubes give the fly rodder maximum stealth. Credit: Cliff Hauptman

pond. You move and steer by kicking your finned feet. Maneuvering a float tube with fins is absolutely instinctive (although climbing into and out of one without embarrassing yourself takes practice). No matter how hard you kick, you will barely chug along, so it's not worth trying to go fast or cover a lot of water. In a tube, you fish slowly and thoroughly, which is the way a bass fly should usually be fished.

Kickboats and pontoon boats come equipped with short oars to supplement kicking your feet so that you can move around a bit more easily and quickly than in a tube, and they put the seat above the water, which makes fly casting easier.

Kayaks are fun to paddle but impractical for the fly-rod bass fisherman. Casting is awkward from that low, sitting position, and the slightest breeze blows the kayak out of position. The best use for a kayak is for moving around a lake or down a river when you intend to stop and get out to fish prime sections of water.

From any one-man watercraft, you can work your way along a shoreline in virtual silence, and your low profile enables you to paddle close to likely cover without spooking fish. You can launch tubes, kickboats, and pontoon boats anywhere you can walk; they are lightweight and easy to carry. Depending on the water temperature, you don't even need to wear waders. A bathing suit keeps you cool on a summer bass pond, althoug if you're leery of leeches or at all spooky about mysterious underwater creatures, you'll be more comfortable in a pair of lightweight waders or quick-drying trousers.

One-man watercraft are ideal for small ponds, sluggish rivers, and other intimate bodies of water whose shorelines feature more-or-less continuous bass cover. They are slow and inefficient, however, wherever you might want to cover a lot of water or move significant distances between hotspots. In even gentle breezes, or in rivers with significant current, maneuvering any one-man watercraft is hard, exhausting work.

Afoot

- *Wading and bank-stalking.* Fly fishing on foot for bass is more trouble than it's worth on the steep, weedy, brush-clogged, mud-bottomed shorelines that characterize much bass water, but wherever the lake or pond bottom is firm and gravelly and gently sloping, and in most smallmouth rivers, fishing unencumbered by any kind of boat is great fun and a good way to catch bass.

  Tiptoe up to the bank and stop well back from the edge. Peer hard into the water before stepping in, to be sure you don't overlook a bass you might catch. Then begin to make short casts in a fanlike pattern, starting parallel to the bank and moving outward with each successive cast. After you

This angler has waded into the pond so he can cast streamers over the dropoff. Credit: Will Ryan

cover that water thoroughly, begin to stalk your way along the shoreline. If you're a right-handed caster, move to your left so that you can keep your line over the water when you cast (and vice versa, of course, if you cast left-handed). Make your targets alleys and potholes in the weeds, underwater rocks, stickups and stubs, dropoffs and depressions in the bottom, and edges of all kinds.

You can cover all the bassy water on foot, and with polarized glasses you can study it better than you can from a boat. Imitate that ultimate fisherman, the heron. If you do a lot of standing still an

Most farm ponds can be fished from the bank. Try to stay low.

looking, you'll rarely spook a fish. You'll enjoy feeling intimate with the water, really getting to know it. It might take you a few hours to cover a hundred yards of shoreline, but you're likely to see lots of bass. Experience will teach you what to look for—shapes, swirls, wakes, shadows, sometimes just a subtle twitch of a reed or movement under a lily pad. If you go slow and watch where you step, you can usually creep up close to them, and you're so low to the water that they can't see you.

A fly cast into the water from the bank gives bass a different, more natural appearance. It behaves the way bass expect it to act. Most bass prey live in the shallow water near the shoreline, and when they panic, they usually head for the weeds or closer to the bank where their cover lies, not into open water.

The best part of going afoot is that you can fish places that no boat can reach—little potholes, creeks, backwaters and ponds, places you have to bushwhack into that are too far from the road even for portaging a one-person craft or a lightweight canoe comfortably.

With waders or hip boots, the angler can bushwack to out-of-the-way bass waters that nobody else fishes.

STEALTH

Whether you travel afoot or by bass boat, rowboat, canoe, or one-man watercraft, if fish know you're there, you're not likely to catch them. Bass are as quick to flee any sudden or unnatural motion, sound, or flash of light as bonefish and trout, especially in shallow water where they feel most vulnerable and where bass fishermen hunt them.

Trout, which always face upstream in moving water, can usually be approached closely from behind; so can river-dwelling bass. But you never know which way a still-water bass might be looking. A few simple precautions will increase your chances of casting to where bass are lurking, not the place from which they've recently fled:

- *Wear drab-colored shirts and hats.* Do this especially when wading or stalking bass from shore. I prefer shades of gray, olive, tan, and brown.
- *Keep a low profile.* You have no choice in a float tube or kickboat, but from a boat you'll hit your targets more regularly if you approach close, remain sitting, and make short casts rather than trying long-distance casts while standing up or perched high on a swivel seat. When wading or prowling the shoreline, move slowly, hunch down, stay in the shadows, and keep bushes or the bank behind you to break up your outline.
- *Avoid noise.* Sound travels a long distance in still water, and bass come with finely tuned sound-

detecting equipment. Just as they will sometimes swim from far away away to investigate something that plops onto the water, so will they flee from the source of any noise that translates as danger.

You can't be absolutely quiet in any boat. Bass cannot hear voices, so you can hoot and holler all you want. You can be sure, however, that every nearby bass will hear the scrape of a foot on the bottom, the bump of a paddle against a gunwale, the clank of an oarlock, and even the buzz of an electric motor. I'm not sure how much particular sounds actually bother bass. I suspect they tolerate some more than others, but any unnatural sound will at least make them nervous. I am quite sure that the best sound of all is silence.

- *Avoid flash and shadow.* Toward sunrise or sunset, when the sun is at a low angle, your long shadow moving across the water will spook fish. Even when your profile and shadow are beyond a bass's cone of vision, there's your fly rod waving high over the water, and if the sun's coming from the wrong angle, fish will be startled by the reflected light. Be aware of the sun and, if necessary, either move to a better position or drop your rod and cast sidearm. Similarly, waving your line over the water can create a moving shadow or flash that will spook shallow-water fish. Make your false casts to the side of your intended target.

- *Beware of scent.* Although bass hunt primarily by sight and sound, any strong unnatural scent will deter them from eating. Particularly noxious to bass are gasoline, insect repellent, sunscreen, and human perspiration. Take the simple precaution of rinsing your hands in the water before handling and tying on your fly.

CHAPTER SEVEN

CATCHING BASS ON FLIES

You've collected an assortment of flies, your gear is assembled, and you've practiced until you're comfortable with it. Now it's time to go catch a bass.

GENERAL TACTICS

- *Still water.* If you're casting toward the shore from a boat, canoe, or one-man watercraft, and you've come upon a bed of lily pads, a big deadfall, or a rocky shoal, the rule of thumb is "outside in." Make short casts to the water nearest you first, then gradually move closer or lengthen your casts. For example, cast first to the outermost tip of a fallen tree, then with successive casts work your way in toward its trunk. This way, the bass you hook on the deep side of the cover will not spook those that are lying closer to the bank. Fish the near edges of a weedbed or shoal or other large bass-holding area before working your fly out over them.

    When fishing from shore, of course, do it the opposite way, that is, inside out. Fish the water closest to you—the base of that fallen tree or the inside edge of the weedbed—before you make longer casts out over deeper water.

- *Moving water.* In rivers and streams, bass, like trout, seek comfortable cushions of soft water

When fishing from a boat, work the outside edges of weedbeds before casting into them. Credit: Will Ryan

close to the swifter currents that carry food—along the banks, near boulders, inside current seams, and in slow-moving pools. Concentrate on these bassy places. You'll often have to cast your fly across fast currents to reach the slower fish-holding water. To keep your streamer or bug in the prime water as long as possible, throw a big upstream mend in your line and move the fly just enough to make it appear alive.

Another effective river tactic is to cover the water methodically. Stripping a streamer or chugging a bug across the current, past boulders and other structure, and over long, slow pools often brings bass zooming up from the bottom. Begin at the head of a pool or run, make an across-and-down

When casting from the shore, fish the water closest to you first.

In rivers, bass seek out the soft water near the banks.

cast, strip the fly back, take two steps downstream, and cast again. When the current creates a big belly in your line, correct it with an upstream mend. A straight line from rod tip to fly enables you to control the movement of the bug across varied currents and to set the hook when a bass hits.

Big hellgrammite or stonefly nymphs should be fished with a dead drift on the river bottom. Nymph fishing for river-dwelling smallmouths works exactly the same as for trout. Make short casts, hold your rod high, and follow the line as it moves downstream. If you don't hook up on the bottom once in a while, it means your nymph isn't getting deep enough. A strike indicator will help you know when a bass has taken your nymph.

SETTING THE HOOK

The importance of keeping your rod pointed at your fly and your line straight during the retrieve and when picking up your line to make another cast is clear. The straight line is equally important when a fish sucks in your fly. By maintaining direct control of your line, you should hook most of the bass that you entice into striking.

Bass have strong jaws. They can clamp down on a fly or leader so hard that even with tension on the line, it won't move in their mouths. Unlike trout and many other fish, bass rarely hook themselves. Before the fish decides to open his mouth and spit out your fly, you must make a hard, positive hook set. This is what tournament fishermen call, inelegantly and, hopefully, inaccurately, "ripping their lips."

When your bug or streamer disappears in a big swirl, resist the impulse to raise your rod tip as you would to hook trout on a small fly and light leader. The rod tip is designed to absorb shock, not to drive a large hook into the bony mouth of a bass. Instead, keep your rod tip pointing at the fish and give a hard pull straight back with your line hand. When you feel the fish's resistance, give it another sharp pull. Then haul up and back with the butt of your rod, using your whole arm not your wrist. This drives home the hook and puts your rod at the proper angle for fighting the fish.

If by chance you fail to hook the fish, attempting to set the hook by pulling straight back on the line rather than heaving with your rod leaves your fly near where the bass took it. Give it a twitch. Mr. Bass might still be there, wondering where that delicious-looking thing went and ready to take another swipe at it.

FIGHTING BASS

Bass are strong and stubborn fighters, but if they're solidly hooked, you should land all of them. Your goal, once you've hooked one, should be to get him in fast, unhook him quickly, and return him to the water before he's exhausted, so that he will recover quickly. This means that you should be aggressive. Don't think of it as "playing" your fish. Take charge. *Fight* him. Force him to come to you.

The trick to fighting a large bass, or any strong fish, is to prevent him from doing what he wants to do. A long, medium-stiff fly rod makes a powerful lever and an efficient fish-fighting tool if you take advantage of it. Keep turning the head of a hooked bass by moving your rod down and sideways in the opposite direction from the one he's chosen. If he wants to burrow deep, lift him. If he heads for a weedbed or other tangle, go "down and dirty," holding your rod low and parallel to the water and using its whole bend to stop and turn him. Don't baby him. The flex of the rod will absorb his surges and prevent him from breaking your leader.

Hooked bass like to jump. When they do, the risk is that they'll fall on the taut leader and tear the fly from their mouths. So when a fish jumps, "bow" to him; that is, bend forward, lower your rod, and push it toward him. This creates enough slack in your line and leader to prevent you and your bass from becoming disconnected.

When you've got a large bass on, it's always a good idea to reel in your slack line and fight him off the reel. Early in the encounter, when he's still strong, he might insist on making a short run. If he's heading for open water, let him go. Hold your rod at about eleven o'clock and make him pull against the bend of the rod and the drag of your reel. That will tire him quickly. When you feel him weaken, pump him in by lifting your rod and reeling in as you lower it.

WHY THE BIG ONES GET AWAY

I have failed to land my share of big fish of many species, including bass, although in my experience, bass are not particularly resourceful or powerful fighters for their size. They like to jump, bulldog, and dive for cover, but they do not make long-distance runs. They tire quickly, and the aggressive angler can usually overpower them. We should never lose a solidly hooked bass.

But we do.

Every time I've hooked and failed to land a big bass, it's been the result of my own carelessness or heedlessness. If he got loose by wrapping the leader around a stub or the anchor line or tangling himself in the weeds, it's because I did not assert myself aggressively enough. If the hook pulled free, I did not set it firmly.

Most of us don't get enough practice fighting really big fish, and these things happen, but there are other reasons for losing fish that are inexcusable. Believe me, I know.

- *Bad knots.* Nothing is more disheartening than feeling your line abruptly go slack in the middle of fighting a large bass, then reeling in and finding your fly gone and a pigtail at the end of your tippet. No well-tied Trilene, Improved Clinch, or other standard angling knot should pull loose. Only badly tied knots fail. Tie them carefully, lubricate them with spit before pulling them tight, and leave a little stub when you clip the end. Test your knots regularly. Pay equal attention to the knot that joins your tippet to the leader and your leader to the line. Don't hesitate to retie dubious knots.
- *Bad hooks.* Check the bend and point of your hook periodically. Keep a file handy for touching up the point and keeping it needle sharp. If you cast aggressively, as you should, your fly will bounce off a rock, dock, or log now and then, which can dull or bend the point and prevent a solid hookup. If you hook a log, tugging to pull your fly free could open the bend of the hook enough to weaken it and let a bass slip free. Once a hook is bent, it's permanently weakened, so rather than trying to bend it back, discard that fly and tie on a new one.
- *Bad tippet.* Encounters with toothy fish like pickerel and pike, a worn or scored tiptop rod guide, and even general wear and tear can create nicked

or frayed spots on your tippet, converting 10-pound-test into 10-ounce. The millimeter of tippet next to the knot connecting it to a heavy bass fly hinges during repeated casting, which will gradually weaken it. "Wind knots" (overhand knots that are usually caused by messed-up casts, not the wind) cut your tippet's strength in half. Run your tippet between your fingertips or, even better, between your lips now and then, and if you feel a nick or wind knot, retie it. It takes only a moment, and tippet material is a lot easier to come by than 5-pound bass. Even if your tippet is sound, retie your fly every hour or so on general principles.

CATCH-AND-RELEASE

I've never eaten a largemouth or smallmouth bass in my life. I've heard that bass from clean, cool water are delicious, and in most waters, keeping a fish for the table now and then will not put a dent in their population. I just feel better putting mine back.

Unless you fish water of questionable purity (and bass can thrive in water you wouldn't want to swim in), there's no reason not to keep a bass for the table now and then. If you enjoy bass fillets, kill and eat the small ones and return the lunkers to the water so they can pass along their trophy genes to the next bass generation. Small ones taste at least as good as big ones, and knowing that a few lunkers still live in your pond definitely leaves a pleasant taste in your mouth.

Catch-and-release is mandated in bass tournaments, and it should also be the general practice of fly fishermen. If you don't know how to fight, land, unhook, and return a bass without injuring or killing him, you don't deserve to catch him.

- *You're the boss.* Fighting a hooked fish aggressively is the first step to assuring him a continued healthy life. The longer he's out there thrashing around on the end of your line, the greater the chance that you'll return him to the water exhausted, susceptible to disease, and easy pickings for a predator. Especially when water temperatures hover around the high end of a bass's comfort zone, a fish "played" to exhaustion might not recover. Nothing saddens the angler (at least this one) more than watching a big fish he's just released turn belly up and sink slowly out of sight. Fighting a fish to death will not happen if you are the aggressor.

  If you're going to be the boss, use reasonably stout leaders (10- or 12-pound-test is plenty stout enough) and a rod with enough backbone to turn the head of a fish who doesn't want to be turned.
- *Use barbless hooks.* Debarb your hooks by mashing down the barbs with pliers. I take care of this before I even clamp a hook into my fly-tying vise. If you buy your bass flies, or if someone gives them to you, debarb them right away. It's one of those steps that you're likely to overlook once you're on the water and eager to start casting.

The best reason for debarbing your hooks is that it enables you to unhook a fish quickly without holding him out of water for a long time or tearing any of his flesh. This will save the lives of fish that inhale your fly and get themselves hooked in the throat or gills or other sensitive parts of their anatomy, which happens quite commonly with bass.

If you fight a fish properly, you will never lose him because your hooks don't have barbs. In fact, barbless hooks penetrate deeper and more easily and give you a higher percentage of solid hookups than those with barbs.

Another considerable benefit of barbless hooks is that you can back them out of the ear or scalp of your partner or yourself without a trip to the hospital.

• *Deeply hooked fish.* Bass tend to inhale their food. When they hit a moving fly, you'll usually hook them in the lip, but when they take a motionless bug off the surface or a streamer dropping between twitches, all too often they get hooked deep in the throat or even in the gills. Setting the hook instantly is not the answer. Usually you'll just pull the fly out of the fish's mouth before he's turned his head and closed his mouth on it.

If he's deeply hooked, or if you've neglected to debarb your hook, reach into his mouth with needle-nosed pliers or long forceps. If the hook is so deep that removing it seems likely to injure the fish, clipping the leader and leaving the fly there gives the fish the best chance for survival. Usually the hook will rust, the fly will work loose, and the fish will be none the worse for the experience.

- *Land him properly.* A wide, long-handled boat net enables you to capture hooked bass quickly and surely, unhook them without excessive handling, and return them safely to the water. There's no need to bring a hooked fish into the boat. Keep the net in the water and simply reach down and back the debarbed hook out.

Because bass do not have teeth, most bass fishermen simply hand-land their fish and don't bother with a net. Never jam your fingers into a fish's gills, grip him by the eye sockets, or squeeze his belly. When you've beaten the fish, raise your rod

After you've fought your bass and he's ready to be landed, lift his head to the surface and drag him toward you . . . Credit: Will Ryan

. . . grab the leader in one hand . . . Credit: Will Ryan

. . . grip his lower lip in the other hand . . . Credit: Will Ryan

. . . lift him from the water so you can unhook him . . . Credit: Will Ryan

. . then use two hands to return him to the water. Credit: Will Ryan

Revive bass in the water before releasing them. Credit: Will Ryan

to lift his head out of the water and drag him to
ward you. Then put down the rod, grab the leade
with one hand, and with the other hand clamp th
bass's bottom lip between your thumb and th

crook of your index finger. This will immobilize him so that you can unhook and release him.

If you're fishing from shore, never drag a bass up onto the bank. This could injure his eyes and gills and will certainly scrape his scales and rub off his protective slime, promoting infection and disease. Land him while he's still in the water, using a net or his convenient lip-handle.

- *Release him quickly.* Fish live underwater. Every second they spend gasping air instead of swimming in the water weakens them and increases their chances of dying. Holding bass out of water, especially in dry, cold weather, will quickly evaporate the natural slime that protects them from bacterial and fungal infections. Handling them excessively under any conditions will destroy their protective slime.

After he's unhooked, use both hands to right the fish in the water. If he seems weak and tired, grip his tail and gently move him back and forth to force water through his gills. Support his belly and keep moving him until you can feel that his strength has returned.

If your bass is bleeding, especially from the gills, when you bring him to the boat, his chances of survival are not good. This is the fish to kill, fillet, bake with bread crumbs, serve with wild rice and a vintage white wine, and eat with ceremonial respect.

CHAPTER EIGHT

WHEN TO GO

Smallmouth and largemouth bass, collectively called "black bass," are first cousins in the *Micropterus* genus of the sunfish family. In temperament, appetite, lifestyle, and behavior, their similarities far outweigh their differences, and for most practical angling purposes, it's sensible to think about smallmouths and largemouths as if they were identical. "Both species," wrote Dr. Henshall over a century ago, "are remarkably active, muscular and voracious, with large, hard and tough mouths; are very bold in biting, and when hooked exhibit gameness and endurance second to no other fish."

For our purposes, both species are equally susceptible to a well-presented bass fly. The word "bass" does the job for both.

Smallmouths and largemouths, of course, are not identical. For one thing, largemouths, um, have larger mouths. They come in shades of gray and black and have a pronounced lateral stripe. Smallmouths, which are called "bronzebacks" by some, have reddish eyes, a greenish-copper coloration, and tend to average a bit smaller than largemouths. There are other, more precise ways to distinguish between them (the size of their scales, the number of spines in their dorsal fins, the shape of their foreheads, etc.), but since both are equally desirable quarry for the bass bugger, who cares which one eats your fly?

WATER TEMPERATURE

The single most important variable in the location, movement, and activity of all cold-blooded creatures is the temperature of their environment. The body temperature of all fish rises and falls along with the temperature of the water around them. They lapse into a semi-comatose state when the temperature rises significantly above or falls much below their comfort range. On the outer extremes of comfortable temperatures, they feed little. In a body of water, or at a time of year, where the water temperature varies in different areas, fish will seek out the most comfortable water.

When the water temperature is ideal, and even when it improves from very uncomfortable to a few degrees less uncomfortable, bass feed most actively.

Smallmouth bass prefer somewhat cooler water temperatures than largemouths do. Credit: Will Ryan

For the bass fisherman, the key to finding and catching bass is understanding how to locate water where the temperatures are closest to ideal.

Largemouths and smallmouths both tolerate a wide range of water temperatures. They can survive in water temperatures from the mid-30s to 90 degrees Fahrenheit, although they like it best when the temperature ranges between 60 and 75 degrees for at least six months of the year. When it drops below 55, the metabolisms of both species slow down, their appetites grow dull, and they are unlikely to hit bass flies on or near the surface. Smallmouths prefer somewhat cooler temperatures—55 to 75 degrees is ideal—and largemouths are most active when the water is between 60 and 80 degrees. Interestingly, however, smallmouths stop feeding almost entirely when the water temperature drops below 50, while largemouths feed sporadically even at the coldest extremes. Unlike smallmouths, largemouths are often taken by ice fishermen.

TIME OF YEAR

The temperature of shallow water is probably the most important key to fishing success for the bass fisherman. When bass find the shallows too cold or too warm, they seek comfort in deep water where you need sink-tip lines, heavily weighted flies, and lots of patience to have a chance to catch them. Fly fishing for bass is a lot more fun, and generally faster sport when the fish are in water 5 feet deep or less.

Generally speaking, both species of bass move to the warm shallows in the springtime, migrate into deeper water in the midday heat of summer, and back to the shallows in the cool of the evening. They favor the shallows as the water cools in late summer and into autumn. Then as winter approaches and the shallow water grows uncomfortably cold, they return to the depths to sulk.

Those times when bass swarm along the shoreline are, of course, prime, and they favor the shallows even in the worst heat of summer. Largemouths thrive year-round in weedy, shallow-water eutrophic ponds and slow-moving rivers, and smallmouths find comfort in cool, oxygen-rich streams. Even when they're lurking around dropoffs, short-term variables such as time of day, weather, wind, and sun keep bass moving into and out of the shallows. Except for winter, there are times throughout the year when you can catch bass on flies.

TIME OF DAY

The old aphorism is a good guide: The most pleasant time of day for the bass angler to be outdoors is also the best time to catch fish:

- On the *margins of the season*, that is, early in the spring and late in the fall, bass seek comfort in sheltered, sun-warmed shallows in the middle of the day, when it's also the most pleasant for the fisherman to be on the water.
- During the *dog days of summer*, bass gravitate to the relative comfort of cool water. They sulk in heavy

In bright summertime sun, bass seek shaded areas. Fishermen who want to catch them should, too.

shade or deep water during the times of high sun, then prowl the shallows to feed in the cool of early morning, late afternoon, evening, and after dark. A few days of soft, refreshing summer rain, or even a heavy cloud cover, might keep them actively prowling the shallows all day. The weather conditions and times of day when shallow water is coolest—those peaceful, magical times for the angler—are when you find bass foraging in shallow water.

- In the temperate months of *late spring and early autumn* when you want to be outdoors all the time, bass are active all day long in bright, as well as shaded, shallow water.
- *Late fall, winter, and early spring* are uncomfortable times for both bass and anglers. A deep

running weighted Clouser might entice an occasional bass, but all but the most obsessive fly fishermen are well advised to take their cue from the bass and hunker down until it warms up.

THE YEARLY CYCLE

Bass, like all organisms, are preoccupied with three powerful survival instincts: to eat, to avoid being eaten, and to procreate. All of their behaviors derive from their instincts to survive as individuals and as a species.

- *The prespawn.* The period immediately preceding spawning time finds bass foraging in the shallows after their long winter of semihibernation. Once

the spring before they begin spawning, bass roam the warm shallows ooking for food.

the water temperature hits about 55 degrees, bass begin feeding heavily to build up their strength for spawning. They prowl the warm shoreline water where their prey, as well as they themselves, are most comfortable, and they gobble bass flies because they're hungry.

- *Spawning season.* In its season, the bass's spawning drive overrides all other concerns. They shed a good deal of their normal wariness in their preoccupation with building and protecting their nests. They feed less, but they become correspondingly more belligerent and attack all invaders of their territory with mindless hostility.

Some fishermen claim to find bass harder to catch when they're spawning. I have found the opposite to be the case, especially with smallmouths. Every bass in the water migrates to the shallows, so they're easy to find. They're also easy to attract. A bug churning up a fuss over their heads or a wiggly streamer darting through their territory screams "Enemy!" and makes bass, especially the males, see red.

The spawning impulse seizes bass when the water temperature approaches 60 degrees, occurring in February or March in the South, and as late as early July in the northern extremes of their range. The fisherman can pinpoint spawning time on any body of water either by using a thermometer or by simply looking for the distinctive round sand-colored beds in water from 2 to 8 feet deep. Drop a fly atop one of those beds, and you're a most guaranteed an angry strike.

Male bass do most of the housekeeping work. They move to the shallows to build their nests while the roe-heavy females linger along the edges of deeper water. After the females have dropped in, laid their eggs, and departed, the males remain behind, first to guard the nests and eventually to attack and disperse their young. Most of the shallow-water bass you'll catch on flies during spawning time will be the smaller, more aggressive males. If you want to go after the larger females, use sink-tip lines and twitch streamers along the edges of dropoffs, although you should think twice about interrupting the important work of the females.

Some anglers refuse to fish when bass are on their spawning beds on the grounds that the fish are too easy to catch and should not, in any case, be disturbed during this all-absorbing process. If you want to protect and conserve the fish, they claim, taking them off their beds is unethical.

Perhaps I am deficient in ethics, but I take a more straightforward and practical approach. Some of my fastest and most memorable bass action has come during spawning time. Sometimes this is not particularly challenging fishing, but sometimes I don't need a challenge to have fun. I focus on the shallow water, and so I hook relatively few of those fat, precious females. I use barbless hooks, fight the fish aggressively, land them quickly, release them unharmed, and return them near where I hooked them. I have caught what I suppose to be the same feisty male bass from the same nest on consecutive days often enough to be convinced that he simply returned to his post and resumed his duty after being hooked, none the worse or wiser for the interruption.

The same ethics that censor fishing during the spawning season should even more logically keep fishermen off the water during the prespawn, when females are on the move and as easy to catch as the males, but I have never heard this argument.

• *The postspawn.* The week or two after the fry disperse and adult bass abandon their beds finds them less interested than normal in eating. Fortunately for the fishermen (and fortunate, too, for the survival of their species), not all bass in any given body of water operate on identical schedules. Some individuals start and complete their spawning earlier than others, and some recover faster than others. Even during the postspawn period, the fisherman can always find a few bass that are willing to inhale a fly.

• *Summer bass.* As late spring moves into summer and spawning is but a vague memory, bass resume heavy feeding, and they don't stop until winter drops the water temperature below their comfort level. When you think of fly-rod bass fishing, you think of summertime.

Anyone who fishes for them regularly has noticed that sometimes summer bass are hungry and active, while at other times they seem lock-jawed. Figuring out when and where to fish is especially challenging during the long summer season.

Fish when you can, of course. Going fishing is always better than the alternatives, but if you have a choice, go when the conditions are most favorable.

In the absence of hard data, I respond to the "feel" of the day. I prefer what I think of as "soft" conditions. Any humid, dark, still summer day beckons me to the water. Usually, the margins of the day, that is, early morning around daybreak and again toward evening, feel "soft." Those are the times when the sun does not blaze upon the

et on the water before dawn for fast summer action. Credit: Will Ryan water and when the wind has not yet come up or has already died down. If a quiet mist is falling, so much the better.

These are the times when the entire body of water seems alive and vital—when bullfrogs grump and grumble, when swallows and bats swoop overhead, when insects buzz and dart and pepper the water, when you can hear the *ker-SLOSH* of a feeding bass around the corner in the next cove. These are also, not coincidentally, the times when water-skiers, speed-boaters, swimmers, and other fishermen are least likely to interrupt the stillness of the place.

I suppose I've acquired this "feel" for soft summer days by having fished obsessively for half a century under every conceivable condition, so that I've internalized the variables that my subconscious associates with fast bass fishing. It does bear up under analysis:

- Bass can see and hear a fly or bug near or on the surface more easily when the water's flat than when it's choppy. Winds from some quarters (no doubt because they're associated with the movement of weather fronts and the changes in barometric pressure, relative humidity, and rising or falling temperatures that accompany them) make for better fishing than others. Generally speaking southerly and westerly winds, at least in the Northeast where I do most of my bass fishing, are preferable to winds out of the east or north. Absolutely no wind is best of all.

- In the summer, both largemouths and smallmouths find *shaded water* cooler and more comfortable than sun-drenched water. Overhanging shoreline bushes, weedbeds, fallen trees, docks, and other sources of shade also protect them from overhead predators, which can spot them less easily in the shade, or anywhere if it's overcast or drizzling. Lake-dwelling smallmouths, which generally seek deeper water as summer temperatures rise, move into shallow water on cool, overcast days.
- Bass are particularly uncomfortable *when bright sun is accompanied by low relative humidity*. Biologists attribute this to the bass's aversion to ultraviolet rays, *not* to light itself. Rain, cloud cover, and even just high relative humidity filter out this

...ass lose their inhibitions when the sun leaves the water and the air ...arts to cool a bit. Credit: Will Ryan

source of discomfort, and under these conditions, bass are less likely to sulk in deep water or dark shade as they tend to do on a bright, dry day. The absence of strong ultraviolet rays explains why dawn and dusk, when the sun does not beat down on the water, are prime bass fishing times. Midday fishing, however—when bass see best—can be quite successful (particularly with subsurface flies), provided that the UV factor is low.

- Bass, like all shallow-water fish, are extremely *sensitive to barometric pressure*. They become active on a falling barometer and grow uncomfortable when high-pressure systems prevail (conditions that feel "hard" to me and dull my enthusiasm for going bass fishing). This accounts for fishing being slow for the first day or two after a cold front moves through and for bass feeding aggressively when a storm is approaching. Fish cannot sense barometric pressure below 10 feet of water, but they are quite sensitive to this variable in the shallows where we prefer to hunt them. In high-pressure conditions, they leave the shallows and migrate to deeper, more comfortable water where a sink-tip line and a weighted fly is your best bet.

- *Bass feed actively at night*, especially during the summer's hottest months, when darkness drops the shallow-water temperature a few degrees after a day of pounding sun. Knowing they can't be seen, bass shed their fear of predators at night and roam the shallows boldly.

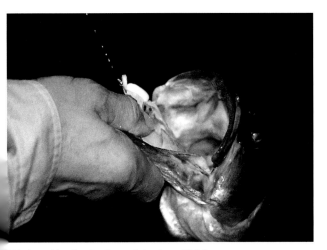
This bass hit a floating bug a little after midnight.

Night fishing in the summertime is prime time for bass bugs. It's arguably the bug fisherman's best chance to catch a truly large bass. Those old survivors are never stupid, but they do tend to shed some of their inhibitions after dark. They hunt more by sound than sight, so a big, noisy bug will attract them.

I know many fishermen who say they've tried fishing for bass at night and have found it disappointing. I suspect they've become discouraged and quit too early. There typically comes a lull in bass activity in the first hour or two after nightfall, and then sometime between ten o'clock and midnight on my New England ponds, the fish seem to become acclimated to the darkness and start foraging. For some reason, they seem to hit better on dark, rather than moonlit, nights.

- *Autumn.* As summer slides into autumn, water temperatures in shallow lakes and ponds begin to drop from the upper limits that bass can tolerate into their comfort zone, and there will be a few weeks when bass feed voraciously to fatten up for their long, semicomatose winter. During this time, they prowl the shallows and along the edges of dropoffs even at midday.

As water temperatures continue to drop, bass increasingly do their feeding where and when they find the most comfortable water—typically along the northern shoreline, which gets daylong sun.

Gradually, water temperatures sink to levels that remind bass it's time to slow down. They retreat to the deep water beyond dropoffs, and bass fishermen stow away their fly rods until next spring.

CHAPTER NINE

WHERE TO GO

Smallmouths are Northern fish. They are associated with deep, rocky lakes and cold, clear-running rivers. We generally think of largemouths, which are native to the Southern states, as fish of warm, weedy, shallow ponds and lakes and of sluggish rivers and backwaters. These generalizations work up to a point.

In fact, the cousins are remarkably adaptable and often coexist in the same water. In lakes that hold both largemouths and smallmouths, they tend to lay claim to different territories: the smallmouths around rocky shoals and boulder-strewn shorelines near

Big smallmouth lakes are best explored by boat. Credit: Fred Bobson

129

dropoffs into deeper water, and the largemouths in shallow, weedy mud-bottomed coves. Many times, however, I have taken one of each species from alongside the same fallen tree or boat dock or boulder on consecutive casts. After more than a century of migration and transplanting, the territories of both species sprawl over most of North America and overlap considerably.

Their differing preferences for types of water, especially the bottom, probably account for the somewhat different preferences the two species exhibit for prey. If smallmouths seem to like crayfish better than largemouths do, for example, it's because crayfish favor the same cool, gravel-bottomed waters that the fish do. Frogs are prime largemouth prey because they like the same kind of water, but both species of bass are confirmed omnivores and will devour crayfish and frogs—and bass flies—with equal voracity whenever they can find them.

If the best *time* to go fishing is *when* you can, then the best *place* to fish is *where* you can. Just as some seasonal and weather conditions increase the likelihood of finding fast fishing, however, so, too, do some bodies of water, and some places on those waters offer better chances than others.

Finding good bass water depends on your definition of "good." For me, ideal bass water meets *all* of these criteria:

- It's *nearby*, which allows me to go on the spur of the moment without a lot of planning and fussing

- It holds a reasonably *large population of bass*, including enough big ones to give me the realistic hope of catching a trophy.
- It's easy for an angler to *fish from shore or launch a canoe or float tube* there, but it provides no direct road access or concrete boat ramps for trailered bass boats.
- It features some combination of steep, brushy banks, weeds, fallen timber, dark coves, and rocky points, with plenty of *shaded shoreline cover* to attract and hold bass and provide interesting casting targets.
- It's *my secret*, and I share it only with my friends.

I've chosen not to compete with the bass-boat fleets, so I no longer fish some of my local bass waters. The truth is bass are just about everywhere, and there's no need to compete. Instead, I've followed rumors, hunches, and topographic maps, and I've found dozens of new places within a half hour's drive of my house. Many of them meet several of my criteria, and a few are close to ideal.

I've found healthy populations of both largemouths and smallmouths in the lower reaches of well-known trout rivers, in streams and brooks that flow into and out of popular bass lakes, in farm ponds and mill ponds, in golf course water hazards, in quarry pits, and even in the tiny reservoirs that New England villagers used to dig to hold emergency fire-fighting water. In fact, I've found very few bodies of water that *don't* hold bass. Some are better than others. It's fun to take their measure.

Many farmers stock their ponds with bass.

Many parts of the country are speckled with tank ponds, canals, irrigation ponds and ditches, duck ponds, and lagoons. Sooner or later, bass seem to appear in almost all man-made bodies of water, even those built for decoration or recreation in housing developments and industrial parks. I've been able to slide my canoe onto many private ponds that offer no public access simply by asking permission, and these waters tend to be lightly fished.

READING THE WATER

Bass do not distribute themselves evenly throughout any lake, pond, or river. On the contrary, they tend to congregate in areas that meet their needs for comfort, food, and protection from predators. Small waters are easier to "read" than big lakes or reservoirs, and if you're illiterate, you can prospect their shorelines blindly until you find fish.

The best way to fly fish for bass is to paddle along parallel to a shoreline and cast toward the bank. A good bass shoreline offers one likely bass hideout after another, which could be the dark cave under an overhanging hemlock, the trunk of a fallen old oak, an alley in the reeds, a pothole in a bed of lily pads, or a jumble of boulders. Much of the mesmerizing allure of bass fishing comes from paddling slowly, combing that shoreline, and hitting the bull's-eye of each of those bassy targets as it comes along. As A. J. McClane wrote, most bass fishing ". . . is done in close to shore among rocks, weed patches, and fallen timber.

Many man-made ponds offer good bass fishing—and are lightly fished.

To me, this is the most interesting way of fishing for bass."

- *Cover and structure.* Structure and cover are not always the same. Cover, that is, weedbeds, fallen trees, overhanging bushes and boat docks, hide bass from overhead predators. Structure can be any kind of underwater object—a stump, rock, piling, or bridge abutment, as well as that fallen tree—or it might be a hump, depression, trough, or dropoff on the bottom. Bass like to lurk alongside and over structure, especially when it's near or under cover. Sonar helps the tournament pros identify subsurface structure, and it would probably help the fly rodder, too. Shoreline fly casting for bass, in contrast, normally requires only the

A weedy cove with fallen timber—classic bass water. Credit: Will Ryan ability to recognize the obvious, because most shallow-water structure and all cover is visible.

You'll often find bass scattered in what appears to be a random way along any shoreline. If you knew what was beneath the surface—a depression on the bottom, a waterlogged tree, a jumble of rocks, a patch of submerged weeds, even an old truck tire—you'd understand that the fish's location wasn't really random at all. By the same token, places that look good to you sometimes come up empty, probably because what's beneath the surface lacks what the bass prefer. In really good-looking bass water, you might actually find more attractive bass-holding targets than there are bass. You'll also come to appreciate the fact that bass, like people, can be fickle and unpredictable. Thankfully, nothing is certain in bass fishing.

- *Edges*. Whether you stick to the shoreline or explore open, deeper water, you'll consistently catch more and bigger bass if you aim your fly for edges, those places where one or more types of holding water rub against each other. Bass gravitate to edges where they can lurk in two or more environments at the same time.

Edges give bass everything they're looking for: protection from predators, comfortable water temperatures, and abundant forage. Typically, a bass will find cover to hide under—the shade of a fallen tree, a weedbed, an overhanging bush, or a boat dock that protects him from the sun and hides him from predators. From there he can keep a

Fallen timber attracts bass.

lookout on the open sunlit water around him, where baitfish or other bass food might appear. He'll dart out of the one environment to snag a meal, or a bass fly, from the other.

Places where several edges meet make prime bass cover. The more edges that converge in a single spot, offering both cover and structure, the better. That's the place to shoot for.

Bass fishing with the fly rod is target shooting. Every cast should have a purpose and a bull's-eye. Purposeful casting is at least half the fun of fly fishing for bass. If you aim for edges and hit them consistently, you'll catch more and bigger bass.

Here are some types of visible edges that the bass fisherman should look for and shoot at:

- *Where any two environments abut.* Bass seek out distinct edges, such as the meeting place of sunlight and shade, riffled and calm water, dark and light bottom, shallow and deep water, open and weedy water, clear and murky water, moving and still water (such as where a stream empties into a pond), cool and warm water (such as a springhole), and two different species of weeds.
- *Weedbeds.* Aquatic vegetation holds everything bass want: cover, structure, and forage. Although bass will scatter themselves underneath any significant patch of floating weeds, more of them will usually lurk along its edges. Lily pads, for example, provide excellent shelter from the sun and from predators. The edges of any weedbed define the meeting place of several environments—sun and shade, shallow and deeper water, weedy and open water, and often two different kinds of bottom. Likewise, the visible alleys and potholes inside a weedbed betray some kind of bottom variation, such as a trench or hole of deep water, a rocky bottom bordering mud, an underwater boulder, or a springhole.
- *Subsurface edges.* Any underwater object that sticks out of the surface signals an underwater edge and makes a likely and easily identified bass-bug target. Bass tend to orient themselves alongside boulders, reeds, stubs, pilings, bridge abutments, and, in fact, anything whatsoever that breaks up their underwater environment.

The classic largemouth hangout is a dead old tree that has toppled into the water and lain there

A steep bank and old bridge abutments—excellent bass water.

for at least a year. Perhaps only a few gnarled twigs poke out of the water, but if the trunk is a foot thick, it takes little imagination to picture the jungle of waterlogged branches under the surface. The water covering that big tree is bassy water indeed. Visualize the tree's underwater borders and rake the whole area thoroughly. A fallen tree creates hundreds of bass-holding edges, combinations of structure and cover that give them excellent places to hide from enemies, avoid the sun, and snipe at minnows, frogs, leeches, and terrestrial creatures. If you take a big bass from a fallen tree, don't be too quick to move along. You might catch three or four more, some even bigger, if you fish it thoroughly and patiently.

- *The borders of the water.* Bass generally avoid the middepths of any body of water. They orient themselves to the water's edges, that is, its surface, bottom, and shoreline. When you cast flies to the shoreline, you are actually casting to fish that are oriented to all three edges. Whenever you target some kind of structure along the shoreline, you're working one of those rich compound edges. If an otherwise likely looking shoreline does not harbor bass, the water is probably too shallow. Look for a shoreline with banks that rise almost straight up from the water. Steep banks usually betray water that's deep enough against the edge to hold bass.

- *Bottom edges.* Study the bottom, as well as the top of the water. Peer down through the surface with polarized glasses and look for places where mud meets silt, silt meets gravel, gravel meets sand—anyplace where the color of the bottom changes. Fish any edges where submerged weedbeds abut open water. A prime bottom edge for smallmouths is along points and shoals where the depth changes abruptly.

- *Moving water.* Bass thrive happily in rivers and streams big and small. Largemouths prefer slow-moving water and typically congregate where the currents are softest, or nonexistent, such as close to brush-clogged banks and in weedy backwaters.

Smallmouths, on the other hand, don't mind moving water. You'll find them in riffles, runs, channels, eddies, pockets, and pools. They

In rivers, smallmouths prefer the slower currents near the bank.

typically orient around midstream boulders. In moving water, smallmouths behave like trout. They always face upstream, and they normally hold a stationary position and wait for the current to bring food to them. At the same time, they don't like to fight heavy currents any more than trout do. Look for them in the comfortable cushions in front of and behind boulders, toward the tail of long, slow pools, in deep channels, in the soft water against the banks, around humps and bowls in the riverbottom, and along current seams.

Under low-light conditions, river smallmouths go on the prowl, and you'll find them foraging on the surface along the shallow edges and near the tailouts of big pools, where a big streamer or a chugging bass bug will bring violent strikes.

The more you understand bass habits and preferences, the better your chances of dropping a fly within striking distance of them. Yet, don't lose sight of the first rule: The best time and place to go bass fishing are when and where you can.

CHAPTER TEN

MORE FLY-ROD FUN

For me, the addictive appeal of bass fishing is that it mostly happens on or near the top of the water where you can see it. You watch your line unfurl over the water, you see your bug or streamer plop down on the water, you watch how it moves when you give it a twitch, and your eyes widen at the sudden swirling hole that opens in the water when a good-sized bass sucks it in.

Largemouth and smallmouth bass are not the only fish that you can catch with bass flies and bass-fishing methods. Bass share their waters with many other worthy species, and it's fun to take advantage of the variety. One of my most memorable days of fishing, in fact, happened one summer afternoon on a slow-moving bass river when I caught eleven different species of fish on the same small Mickey Finn streamer.

- *Panfish.* I have never fished a warmwater pond, lake, or river for largemouths where I didn't find sizable populations of sunfish such as bluegills, pumpkinseeds, or longears. These platter-shaped small-mouthed fish like to nudge and tug at a twitched bass-sized fly. If you're getting a lot of tugs and nibbles but aren't hooking anything, chances are your fly is attracting sunfish that, try as they might, just can't get it into their mouths.

There are few largemouth waters that don't harbor healthy populations of hard-fighting bluegills.

Specimens large enough to take a bass-sized hook into their mouths fight as hard for their size as bass and provide incidental fun for the bass-bug fisherman. But it doesn't have to be incidental. I know a pond where there's a healthy population of giant bluegills the size of small dinner plates, and the largemouths run small. There I fish exclusively for bluegills with small bugs or Woolly Worms, and I'm happy to catch the occasional bass.

When the bass fishing is slow, or anytime you crave a couple of leisurely hours of no-pressure, low-tech fishing with the absolute guarantee that you'll catch some fish, tie on a panfish-sized bug or nymph. Anything that can fit into a bluegill's mouth will catch them, but a foam slider or a buggy nymph, provided it's armed with wiggly rubber legs or hackle and tied on a Size 8 hook, works best.

Anytime you find yourself needing an hour or two away from it all, string up your trout-weight fly rod, stick a few panfish bugs or nymphs in your hat brim, tuck a spool of 3X tippet in your shirt pocket, roll up your pants legs, and walk or wade around the margins of your local mill pond. Cast your fly where you'd cast for bass, such as along the edges of weedbeds, under overhanging shoreline bushes, and against fallen trees, then give it a twitch, let it rest, and twitch it again. Sunfish and bluegills suck in their food, and you'll hook them consistently if you pause for a couple of counts before setting the hook. With their broad flanks, even small ones pull hard; and don't be shocked if you catch a 4-pound largemouth once in a while.

Crappies are almost as ubiquitous as the various sunfishes. They are schooling fish that typically feed under the surface on shiners and minnows and a trout-sized streamer in chartreuse, yellow, or white is deadly. I have also caught many crappies some of them as big as pie plates, on bass bugs.

Yellow and white perch, like crappies, are primarily minnow eaters, although they happily eat nymphs and leeches when they're available. I have never caught a perch on a surface fly, though

Crappies are minnow eaters that readily take surface flies. Credit: John Likakis

I've caught thousands of them in my life. Perch are schooling fish; where you find one, you're likely to find a couple dozen. Perch take small streamers readily. If you enjoy eating fish, take an hour or two out of a day of bass fishing to catch a mess of perch, which, many believe, are the most delicious of all freshwater fish, especially those you take from cool, clean water.

Panfishing with a small floater or nymph is, hands down, the best way to introduce a kid to the fun of fly fishing. Panfish are aggressive and forgiving, and they pull hard. Graduating from bluegill fishing to bass fishing is an easy step.

• *Pickerel and pike.* These razor-toothed cousins are aggressive predators that attack bass-sized streamers and chugging bass bugs with heart-stopping ferocity. Pickerel are found in most largemouth waters, while pike, which prefer somewhat cooler water temperatures, often coexist with smallmouths. Look for both species in weedy coves, along the outside edges of weedbeds, and around fallen trees.

Pike and pickerel are fish eaters. They have wide, toothy mouths, and they are built for speed. When they zero in on a streamer or a bug, you'll often see a hump in the weeds and then a torpedo-like wake moving behind your fly.

These fish prefer long, sinewy flies. All yellow, yellow and red, and red and white are the best colors. Fish the fly fast and keep it moving, and when you see a wake materialize behind it, don't slow it down.

Northern pike eat big bass bugs and streamers.

Add a foot of hard 40-pound-test monofilament to the end of your leader. It won't discourage pike or pickerel from striking your fly, and it will prevent them from slicing through your tippet.

We've come a long way since those old Seminoles dabbed their bushy bobs over the weedy surface of Everglades lagoons from the bow of a dugout canoe. We've learned a lot about bass, we've refined our equipment, we've invented scores of flies, and we've cast them on waters all over North America.

But fly rodding for bass remains essentially the same. It's still an effective way to catch them, and it's always lots of fun.

INDEX